CHARTS OF

APOLOGETICS

AND

CHRISTIAN EVIDENCES

Books in the Zondervan*Charts* Series

CHARTS OF

APOLOGETICS

AND

CHRISTIAN EVIDENCES

H. Wayne House
Joseph M. Holden

ZONDERVAN

Charts of Apologetics and Christian Evidences
Copyright © 2006 by H. Wayne House

Requests for information should be addressed to:

Zondervan, 3900 *Sparks Dr. SE, Grand Rapids, Michigan* 49546

Library of Congress Cataloging-in-Publication Data

House, H. Wayne.
    Charts of apologetics and Christian evidences / H. Wayne House and Joseph M. Holden.
        p. cm. – (Zondervan charts)
    Includes bibliographical references.
    ISBN 978-0-310-21937-8
    1. Apologetics — Charts, diagrams, etc. I. Holden, Joseph. II. Title.
    BT1107.H68 2006
    239.022'3 — dc22

                                                                                    2006030875

Interior design: Angela Eberlein

Printed in the United States of America

To Michael J. Adams
In appreciation for his friendship
"There is a friend who sticks closer than a brother."
PROVERBS 18:24

To David Joseph Holden
My beloved son, who was graciously given
as a gift from the Lord.
PSALM 127:3

Contents

Preface

The defense of the Christian faith has come on rough times in recent days. Part of this is due to the negative view, or caricature, of apologists defending the faith who sometimes have been less than charitable with those with whom they disagree. Forgetting the admonition of Peter to be able to give a defense for the hope within us with meekness and fear (1 Peter 3:15), some have sought to figuratively slay the opponent. Another reason for the seeming lack of emphasis in apologetics relates to a post-modern or existential mind-set in which truth as an objective reality is really not knowable; everyone has their own truth, rather than truth being the same for everyone.

Now, more than ever, there is need for works on apologetics. In this small contribution, we have sought to present in clear, logical, and organized form, and in a manner that reflects evenhandedness toward differing perspectives, the various categories relating to apologetics. These categories cover the gamut of general apologetics: methodology, philosophy, theistic arguments, religious theory, the Bible, and science. We did not include cultural apologetics, which relates more to ethical matters. Defense of the Christian faith happens on all of these intellectual fronts, and we have attempted to approach various ways in which the faith may be defended with arguments that many apologists have used.

The book is divided into clearly discernable categories. In apologetic methodologies we discuss ways in which various apologists have approached their task, matters of presuppositions, perspective of the relationship of faith and reason, evidence of different apologists and apologetic methods in the Bible and in church history. In the section on philosophical apologetics we speak of the legitimacy of philosophical inquiry into truth, the tools used by philosophers that are necessary to the apologetic task, the nature of truth, use of logic, and other such topics. The section on theistic apologetics includes the traditional arguments for the existence of God, possible explanations for the problem of evil, differing views on the nature of God, and sets forth worldview differences. Religious apologetics relates to the broader debates outside the Christian community, generally, and concerns the nature of religion and the viewpoints of various world religions, in contrast to Christian thought. In the section on biblical apologetics we explore the attacks on Christianity that attack the Bible. We present the various arguments given against the trustworthiness and authority of the Bible and provide evidence from textual transmission, history and archaeology, and critical studies that the Bible presents truth claims and is reliable. Moreover, we deal with charges against the historicity of the person, words, and works of Jesus made from certain critical circles by some contemporary New Testament scholars, including the important question of the resurrection of Christ and the case for miracles. The last section deals with how science and the Bible relate. We provide the different arguments on evolution and creation, alternate creation theories within the Christian community, and evidence on the question of intelligent design.

The reader should not be able to discern the particular view of the authors in most of the charts, since our goal was only to be descriptive of the positions and arguments made by apologists or, at times, those whom apologists argue against, as in the world religious perspectives. In other cases, we provide helpful facts that support the Christian view, such as historical, archaeological, or philosophical information that supports the Christian faith.

It is our hope that the readers of this book will be encouraged to be involved in the apologetic task, which is to demonstrate the truthfulness of the Christian religion in a world of religious confusion, and that by so doing many people will embrace the one who is the Truth, the Way, and the Life—Jesus Christ.

H. Wayne House
Joseph M. Holden

Soli Deo Gloria!

Acknowledgments

Over the years one accumulates much information from a variety of sources, some written, some in lectures and talks, some in classes one teaches, and others in private conversation. This book reflects such a process. Many of these charts developed and have been tested over the years by the interaction of students in various classes we have taught. We give them thanks for their insight and critique. Other charts were developed as we read different authors and gained from their arguments. We thank them for their words and hope that we have properly given credit to each of them. Both of us have benefited from the fine example of many Christian apologists over the years, but particularly from Norman Geisler, whose acumen, clarity of thought, and wit have been a good example to us. We regret that many of those who have been on the other side of the debate with him have not also been in private with him to see his humility, fairness, and humor. He truly argues against the viewpoint that places itself in contradiction to the truth, not against the person.

We wish to express appreciation to Joel Wingo for his help with research assistance and to Calvary Chapel Bible College for the use of their facilities in completing this project. Special thanks to Eddie Colanter for his contribution to charts on miracles and intelligent design. Any person that we have failed by our oversight to acknowledge we offer our heartfelt regrets and ask for forgiveness.

PART 1
APOLOGETIC
METHODOLOGIES

What Is Apologetics

Definition	Apologetics is the branch of theology that offers a rational defense for the truthfulness of the divine origin and the authority of Christianity. In the classic sense of the word, "apologetics" derives its meaning from the Greek word *apologia*, which means "defense." A judicial term, it describes the way a lawyer deliberately and rationally presents a verbal defense of a particular claim. Or, more precisely, apologetics is to "speak away" (*apo* = away, from; *logia}* = speech, word) the charge brought against an individual (Acts 25:16; 19:33; 22:1; 1 Corinthians 9:3; 2 Corinthians 7:11; 1 Peter 3:15; Philippians 1:7, 16; 2 Timothy 4:16).
Aspects of Apologetics	Within the apologetic task of defending the faith there emerge at least two distinct aspects. The destructive aspect seeks to "dismantle" or explain away arguments against Christianity (2 Corinthians 10:3–5; Titus 1:9–11). The creative aspect offers evidence and proofs to support arguments for the truthfulness of the Christian faith (Acts 1:3; Luke 24:39; Romans 1:19–20).
Ancient Use of Apologetics	In secular society, the use of apologetics as a defense against an attack occurred as early as the 5th century BC when Socrates presented his own defense before an Athenian court, which was later chronicled by his student Greek philosopher Plato in *The Apology*. During the 1st century AD, Josephus offered an apologetic on the ancient origin of the Jewish religion in his *Against Apion* (AD 93–95). In the early years of the church, Justin Martyr (100–167) and Tertullian (155–235) are recognized as apologists through their writings—*First Apology* and *Second Apology* by Martyr and *Apologeticum* by Tertullian. Among other early apologists were Tatian, Athenagoras, and Theophilus. Their main task, as Christianity sought to gain acceptance as a legitimate religion within the Roman Empire, was to defend Christianity against attacks from Roman philosophical society and pagan religious culture. Irenaeus defended the faith (*Against Heresies*) against Gnostic ideas that emanated from within the church.
Biblical Use of Apologetics	The principal Scripture for describing and advocating apologetics is 1 Peter 3:15, which says, "But sanctify the Lord God in your hearts, and always being ready to give a defense to everyone who asks you a reason for the hope that is in you, with meekness and fear." Several examples are seen in Scripture, such as Elijah confronting the prophets of Baal in 1 Kings 18 in order to demonstrate Yahweh as the Most High God; God giving Moses evidence that God would speak through him (Exodus 4); Stephen giving a defense of his faith before his persecutors (Acts 7); Paul arguing for his faith before kings, magistrates, and philosophers (Acts 17; 22); and Jesus defending His claims against challenges of the Pharisees and Sadducees (Matthew 22:34–46; John 5).

Chart 1

Why Christians Often Reject Apologetics

- They consider themselves theologically ill-equipped or socially insecure.

- They have a fear of or are uncomfortable with confrontation or debate.

- They confuse arguments on issues with attacks against a person.

- They have a preoccupation with accentuating the positive and downplaying the negative.

- They believe apologetics is ineffective in evangelism.

- They assume that apologists believe reason and evidence can save someone.

- They have created an improper dualism between faith and reason.

- They assume that the improper manner/attitude of some apologists invalidates the apologetic task.

Chart 2

Apologetics in Scripture

Old Testament		
Individuals Involved	**Scripture**	**Occasion**
God and Moses	Exodus 4:1–9	God gives Moses the signs of the miraculous rod and the instantaneous transformation of the leprous hand to confirm His message.
Moses and Aaron	Exodus 7:8–13	Miraculous rod confirms Moses' and Aaron's credentials.
Moses	Exodus 7:17–12:30	Plagues of Egypt are a sign to Pharaoh.
Elijah	1 Kings 18:20–40	Elijah provides evidence to Ahab and the prophets of Baal that Yahweh is the true God.
God and Israel	Isaiah 1:18	God calls Israel to reason with Him regarding their spiritual condition.
God	Isaiah 48:3–5	God gives prophecy as an apologetic for His unsurpassed greatness.
Moses and Korah	Numbers 16:1–35	God gives evidence to the people that Moses is God's choice to lead Israel by removing Korah supernaturally.
New Testament		
God	Genesis 1:1 Romans 1:19–21	God gave His creatures evidence of His existence and nature through what was created.
Holy Spirit	John 16:7–11	The Holy Spirit will convict the world of sin, righteousness, and judgment.
Jesus	Matthew 22:23–33 Mark 2:10–11 Luke 24:39 John 5:17–39 John 11:41–44 Acts 1:3	Jesus defends His identity as Lord, His ability to forgive sins, His resurrection from the dead, His equality (deity) with the Father. and His mission as Messiah. Luke describes Jesus as showing Himself by many "infallible proofs."
Mark	Mark 16:20	The Lord confirmed the message with accompanying signs and wonders.

Chart 3

Apologetics in Scripture (continued)

Peter	Acts 2:22 Acts 2:14–36 1 Peter 3:15–16	The miracles prove the claims of Jesus. Peter defends the manifestation of tongues at Pentecost. Peter commands Christians to give a defense of their hope in Christ.
Peter and John	Acts 4:18–20	The apostles defend their right and duty to preach the gospel.
Paul and Barnabas	Acts 14:6–20	They gave evidence for God and said idolatry was worthless.
Paul	Acts 17:1–3; 19:8 Acts 17:16–34 Acts 22:1ff Acts 24:1–27 2 Corinthians 10:3–5 2 Corinthians 12:12 Philippians 1:7, 16 2 Timothy 2:24–25 Titus 1:9–11	Paul reasoned and persuaded the religious Jews, gave evidence to the Stoic and Epicurean philosophers that God ought to be worshiped and that Jesus was resurrected from the dead, defended his ministry to the Jewish mob at Jerusalem, defended the gospel against charges before Governor Felix, declared that ideas that are against Christ ought to be dismantled and brought into conformity to Christ, and offered the "signs of an apostle" to defend his calling. Paul's mission was to defend the gospel of Jesus Christ. Timothy was encouraged to correct those in opposition to sound knowledge that God may lead them to repentance. Titus was told to refute teachings that are contradictory to the gospel.
Unknown author	Hebrews 2:3–4	Signs and wonders offered to confirm the gospel.
Stephen	Acts 6:9–7:60	Stephen defended against the charge of blasphemy brought against him at Jerusalem.
Jude	Jude 3	Believers are to contend for the faith.

Chart 3

Reasons for and against Apologetics

Reasons *for* Apologetics	Reasons *against* Apologetics
Apologetics is a biblical command (1 Peter 3:15).	Apologetics devalues the gospel message since "without faith it is impossible to please Him" (Hebrews 11:6; Romans 1:16).
Christians are to contend for the faith (Jude 3).	The Bible is like a lion, it will defend itself (Hebrews 4:15).
Christians are to pull down strongholds that stand against Christ (2 Corinthians 10:4).	It is the Holy Spirit's work to convict and persuade the heart of the sinner (John 14).
Christians are to eliminate doubts in the mind of the convert (2 Corinthians 10:5).	Paul decried the use of worldly wisdom for the purpose of convincing the unbeliever (1 Corinthians 2:1–5, 13).
Christians are to give a reason for their hope in Christ (1 Peter 3:15).	Human reason has been affected by the sin nature and cannot reason correctly (1 Corinthians 2:14; Ephesians 2:1).
False doctrines and ideas should be addressed (Titus 1:9–11).	We are commanded to love our enemies and told that the gates of hell would not prevail against the church (Matthew 5:44; 16:18).
God uses reason to argue His case (Isaiah 1:18).	God's ways are higher than our ways and His thoughts higher than our thoughts (Isaiah 55:9).
Without evidence it is unreasonable to believe (Luke 24:39; Hebrews 11:6); God gave mankind evidence of His existence and nature in creation (Romans 1:19–21).	Reasons and evidence cannot save anyone (Romans 10:9–10; Ephesians 2:8–9). The material creation is under the curse and does not adequately reflect God's nature (Romans 5; 8:20).
Jesus as well as Paul and other Christians engaged in apologetics (Matthew 22; Acts 17; 18:24–28).	The Gospels and Acts are historical narratives which are descriptions of what happened, not directions for what must happen today.
Christianity is under attack from outside and inside the church.	To defend against theological attack demonstrates a lack of faith in God's power to preserve the church.
It is impossible to argue against apologetics, since one would have to use apologetics to do so.	A simple denial, without arguing against the validity of apologetics, is not a defense tactic.

Chart 4

Apologetics in the Early Church

Apologist	Date	Apologetic Works	Apologetic Approach
Aristides	2nd century	*Apology*	Divided mankind into groups of barbarians, Greeks, Jews, and Christians; argued for the superiority of Christianity.
Justin Martyr	AD 100–167	*First Apology* *Second Apology* *Dialogue with Trypho*	Defined the nature of being a Christian, contrasted Christianity with paganism, argued against Judaism, and was the first to call the church the "new Israel."
Tatian	2nd century	*An Address to the Greeks*	Outspoken critic of Greek culture and religion who claimed that Christianity was older and morally superior.
Athenagoras	2nd century	*A Plea for the Christians* *On the Resurrection from the Dead*	Defended Christianity against charges of atheism, cannibalism, and incest. Argued for the resurrection of the dead.
Theophilus	2nd century	*Ad Autolycum*	Sought to persuade his friend Autolycus concerning the truth of Christianity. He addressed such topics as God, interpretation of the Old Testament, and the moral superiority of Christianity.
Irenaeus	AD 120–203	*Against Heresies*	Attacked the Gnostic heresies and systematically refuted then current heretical doctrines that challenged the church.
Clement of Alexandria	2nd–3rd centuries	*Exhortation to the Heathen* *Stromata* *Paedagogus*	Demonstrated the superiority of Christianity over Greek mythology, philosophy, and mystery cults.
Tertullian	AD 155–235	*Apologeticum* *Against Marcion* *Against Heretics* *Against Hermogones*	As a lawyer skilled in the practice of Roman law, he has been credited with expanding the Latin ecclesiastical vocabulary by hundreds of words in his defense of Christianity. He vigorously defended Christianity against the charge of atheism and offered arguments to establish the existence and worship of the one true God through the use of the Bible, fulfilled prophecy, and an appeal to public historical records.
Origen	AD 185–253	*Against Celsius* *On First Principles*	His defense of Christianity is broad in scope, touching on issues such as the deity of Christ, prophecy, the problem of evil, the resurrection of the body, and the functions of angels and demons. He defended the faith against philosophical, historical, and scientific assaults.
Athanasius	AD 296–373	*Against the Heathen* *On the Incarnation of the Word* *Letters Concerning the Holy Spirit*	His apologetic approach is largely christological as he argues for fulfilled messianic prophecies, the resurrection, and the incarnation of Christ. Athanasius defended against idolatry in association with the gods of Greek polytheism.
Augustine	AD 354–430	*Of True Religion* *The City of God* *Confessions* *On the Freedom of the Will* *Against Two Letters of the Pelagians* *On the Correction of the Donatists*	Augustine's apologetic was broad and comprehensive, involving arguments for the existence of God, morality, the nature of time, memory, truth, sin, and salvation.

Chart 5

The Relationship between Faith and Reason

Proponents	Time Period	Explanation
Plato and Aristotle	428–322 BC	Both philosophers developed versions of natural theology (consideration of the natural world to understand the truths of God) by showing how religious beliefs emerge from rational reflections on concrete reality. An early form of religious apologetics, demonstrating the existence of gods, can be found in Plato's *Laws*. Aristotle's *Physics*, from evidence of motion in the world, offers arguments demonstrating the existence of an unmoved mover as a timeless self-thinker.
Plotinus	AD 205–270	In his work *Enneads*, Plotinus describes the One as beyond multiplicity and prior to being, and though necessarily existing, remaining beyond being and any positive description. The individual knows the One by what it is not, predominantly by observing reality, which is characterized by multiplicity (i.e., many things). Therefore, knowledge of the Ultimate is through the *via negativa* (way of negation), or negative knowledge (e.g., the one is not the many).
Tertullian	160–220	As a Christian and a lawyer, Tertullian engaged in the defense of Christianity from both faith and reason. Despite his stress on faith, rationality was by no means discarded, since he viewed the natural world as a means by which to gain knowledge of God's existence and character as a rational being.
Augustine	354–430	Although in some of his works Augustine appears to have believed that intellectual understanding follows from faith (*On the Creed*), at other times he seems to have identified a place for reason and understanding prior to faith (*On Free Will; Letters*). Since Augustine changed several of his theological views during his career, it seems best to allow both faith and reason a prominent position within their respective domains. Faith appears to be salvifically prior to reason in that the principles of salvation cannot be extracted from a purely rational inquiry. However, reason is epistemologically (i.e., in the understanding process) prior to faith since one must hear and evaluate the gospel message prior to placing belief in Christ.
Anselm of Canterbury	1033–1109	Anselm held that the natural theologian (who considers the natural world to understand the truths of God) seeks not to understand in order to believe, but to believe in order to understand. This is not to say that Anselm was a fideist, relying on faith instead of reason. The opposite is true since he offered proofs for the existence of God (e.g., ontological and cosmological arguments; *see chart 28*) and believed Christianity could be defended with reason (*Cur Deus Homo* 1.1; 2.22). Perhaps it is best to view Anselm as one who saw reason as an inadequate means or cause of salvation, but employed it in the defense and understanding of Christianity.
Thomas Aquinas	1225–1274	Aquinas distinguished between faith and reason without making a complete separation. He believed that faith is founded upon God and the Bible, although there are intellectual reasons to render one's belief credible to others, including unbelievers. Within Christianity there are certain doctrines (e.g., the incarnation of Christ) that cannot be proven by natural reason and must be adopted by faith. Other things, such as God's existence, can be proven through rational argument (e.g., the "five ways").

Chart 6

The Relationship between Faith and Reason (continued)

Peter Lombard	1100–1160	Lombard argued that pagans can know truths about God simply by the possession of reason.
William of Ockham	1285–1347	Although William was a theist, believing in God as creator, he offered those of the late Middle Ages a decidedly skeptical approach to apologetics and knowledge. He insisted that one cannot know God through deductions based on observations or experience, because the senses must be distrusted. He insisted that intuition, or faith, is the best way to know that God exists. Only through faith can one know God's attributes, the immortality of the soul, and human freedom of the will.
Martin Luther	1483–1546	Luther's approach to faith and reason appears to be complete dismissal of reason as it applies to matters of faith. However, this view is mistaken. Luther appeared to stress only the limits of reason as it pertains to salvation—that reason cannot save anyone, salvation is only by God's grace through faith alone. According to Luther, reason can be informative when contemplating how best to approach the mundane circumstances of life, but cannot reveal spiritual doctrines. Before faith, reason is in darkness to divine matters; after faith, reason can be used as an excellent instrument of piety by making speech clear and eloquent. Reason receives life from faith and ultimately can illuminate spiritual matters (faith).
John Calvin	1509–1564	Although human reason obfuscates God's revelation in nature, there is an intuitive awareness of divinity. Ultimately, faith is not against reason, rather it is beyond human reason.
John Locke	1632–1704	Locke's aim was to demonstrate the reasonableness of Christianity. Though faith and reason have distinct domains, faith must be in accord with reason. Faith cannot convince us of what contradicts our knowledge. Yet propositions of faith are, nonetheless, understood to be "above reason."
David Hume	1711–1776	Hume argued that concrete experience (i.e., through our five senses) is "our only guide in reasoning concerning matters of fact." His radical approach eliminates any statement that is not true by definition or verifiable with at least one of our five senses. Hume rejected the possibility of arguing for the truths of faith on the basis of natural theology (consideration of the natural world to understand the truths of God) or the evidence of miracles since neither falls into his two categories of proof (*Enquiries Concerning Human Understanding* and *Concerning the Principles of Morals*, 12.3.132ff.).
Immanuel Kant	1724–1804	Although he believed in God, Kant rejected the notion that human reason could know the unseen realm, of which God is a part. Knowledge is relegated to what is observable, thus eliminating the traditional arguments for the existence of God used in Christian apologetics. Instead, God can be accepted and understood by faith since it helps one make sense of the moral world (*Critique of Pure Reason*).

Chart 6

Types of Focus in Apologetics

Focus	Explanation	Proponents[1]
Philosophical	Interacts with areas such as logic, reality, truth, knowledge, morality, semantics, and foundational principles.	Thomas Aquinas C. S. Lewis William Lane Craig J. P. Moreland
Theistic/ Theological	Focuses on systems of theology that challenge Christianity's essential elements: the existence and nature of God, the incarnation, the problem of evil, the resurrection of Christ, and the atonement.	Thomas Aquinas Norman L. Geisler
Biblical	Defends the historical reliability, revelational nature, and inerrancy of Scripture. Biblical apologetics solves internal difficulties (apparent contradictions in the Bible) and defends those biblical truths known only through special revelation, such as the deity of Christ and the Trinity.	B. B. Warfield Don Stewart
Historical	Studies the historical development and relationships between heresy and Christian doctrine. Ancient extra-biblical sources such as Tacitus, Suetonious, and Josephus are evaluated.	John W. Montgomery Gary Habermas
Cultural	Interacts with societal trends in matters of ethics, government, family, and religion.	Francis Schaeffer William Watkins
Scientific	Defends Christianity from arguments that attempt to position the scientific domain against Christianity.	Henry Morris Duane Gish Hugh Ross Phillip Johnson William Dembski

[1] Inclusion of various proponents does not mean that a particular type does not have other foci in apologetics, only that these are the main emphases.

Chart 7

General Apologetics Systems

System	Approach	Criticism	Response	Proponents
Evidential	Defends and supports Christianity as factual by applying historical evidence, including archaeological, bibliographical, and experiential evidence as well as rational evidence (philosophical reasoning with no need for empirical support, as when showing logical contradictions in statements). Truth claims of Christianity are believed to be reasonable and highly probable, though most evidentialists believe there are no indisputable historical facts. Evidentialists use a "one-step" approach that demonstrates both God's existence and which variety of theism is true.	Empirical evidences are interpreted through presuppositions and the framework of one's worldview and therefore should be offered after the philosophical considerations have been addressed.	Evidence is not necessarily presented as "self-evident" conclusive verification; rather it gives good reason and high probability for one to conclude that the truths of Christianity are consistent with the facts. Many philosophical arguments, such as those offered to demonstrate God's existence (e.g., cosmological and teleological arguments; *see chart 28*), present premises which must be supported by empirical evidence.	Thomas Aquinas William Paley John W. Montgomery Joseph Butler Edward Carnell Bernard Ramm Josh McDowell B. B. Warfield Charles Hodge Norman L. Geisler
Presuppositional	The presuppositional approach starts by assuming Christian truth about God and Jesus Christ as revealed in Scripture and reasons *from* Christianity. The presuppositionalist apologetic to the unbeliever begins by reasoning "from" Christianity through special revelation (Bible). The presuppositionalist assumes the content revealed in Scripture to be true and encourages the unbeliever to do the same since these assumed biblical truths offer the only possible foundation and explanation for life and godliness—a framework on which to make sense of the world and God the way they actually exist. Due to the effects of sin, the unbeliever's presuppositions are deemed irrational and inadequate to understand or explain the basis for religion, morals, communication, even beauty. In some instances presuppositionalists test consistency by using laws of logic. The goal is to demonstrate, in any of several ways, that only biblical presuppositions provide the tools for one to make sense of reality and show that Christianity offers the only foundation and framework on which to make sense of the world and God.	Presupposing the truth of Christian theism is arguing in a circle and lacks a basis to justify its assumptions as to why one should presuppose Christianity. The apostle Paul says that God's existence and attributes can be "clearly seen" (Romans 1:18–20) since they have been "shown" to the unbelieving world through "the things that are made" (nature). Therefore, the unbeliever's problem is not one of not *understanding* the truth of God, but of suppression, which leads to not *receiving* the truth.	The presuppositional basis is not circular since its argument is transcendental, which demonstrates that proof is possible only because of God's existence.	Cornelius Van Til John Frame Gordon Clark Greg Bahnsen Abraham Kuyper Herman Bavinck

Chart 8

General Apologetics Systems (continued)

System	Approach	Criticism	Response	Proponents
Fideistic/ Experiential	Belief is that apologetics should be accomplished by faith, not by fallen man's reason. Often describes Christianity as "beyond, above, or against" reason. One's theological knowledge of God is discovered in the Scriptures and can only be engaged and applied by faith. No rational justification or proof is necessary. Some of Christianity's concepts and doctrines are said to be inexpressible and unintelligible for the human mind. Fideistic apologetics engages in both negative and positive aspects of apologetics. Negatively, fideism asserts that the use of rational argumentation is insufficient to reason for Christianity; positively, it argues for the sufficiency of faith to discover and answer theological challenges.	Fideism is inconsistent, if not contradictory, on biblical and philosophical grounds. Throughout Scripture God encourages the use of reason regarding spiritual matters (Isaiah 1:18; 1 Peter 3:15). How can one believe in God without first believing that He exists (Hebrews 11:6)? A rational defense of fideism appears contradictory since reason is employed to suggest one should not use reason to defend Christianity.	Reason cannot be the basis for salvation or faith; God must be the basis. To the human mind, reason is inadequate to enable belief. Only God through the Holy Spirit can bear witness to a person's conviction and confirmation of the Word of God and Christ as Savior as well as the decision to receive Christ, a completely subjective event.	Martin Luther Søren Kierkegaard Karl Barth
Classical	Operates in a two- or three-step process (philosophical, theistic, and evidential). Working from the vantage point of certain undeniable foundational principles, such as the laws of logic and self-existence, certain philosophical questions are addressed, such as truth, reality, meaning, and morality. Since a belief in God as creator is essential for an individual to become a Christian (Hebrews 11:6), the primary goal is to help the unbeliever understand reality untainted by any false assumptions. The second step offers evidence for the existence of God, usually in the form of traditional theistic arguments and empirical data such as manuscript and archaeological evidence.	Overemphasis on reason appears to make an infinite God subject to logic and finite human reason, thus devaluing Christianity. God's ways are higher than our ways and His thoughts higher than our thoughts and therefore man should not try to intellectually comprehend Him (Isaiah 55:8–9).	God is not subject to our logic or finite human reason; only man's theories and propositions about Him need to be tested by the rules of thought. Though God's ways and thoughts are beyond our finite reason, they are not contrary to reason (Isaiah 1:18; 1 Timothy 6:20).	Augustine Thomas Aquinas C. S. Lewis William Lane Craig Norman L. Geisler J. P. Moreland

Chart 8

Evidential versus Presuppositional

Note: These two systems of apologetics are mutually exclusive approaches, whereas the other systems in chart 8, "General Apologetics Systems," are complementary approaches, often borrowing from each other's methodology. Evidentialism reasons *for* or *to* Christian truths; presuppositionalism reasons *from* Christian truths.

	Evidential	Presuppositional
Nature of Man (Depravity)	Depravity is total, it is extensive (to every part), but not intensive (not rendering mankind's faculties unresponsive to God)	Depravity is total, it is extensive (to every part), and it is intensive (rendering every human faculty unresponsive to God)
Image of God	Damaged in man	Damaged in man
Spiritual Death	Likened to "sickness," "blindness," and "impurity"	Likened to a corpse
Unregenerate Mind	Able to perceive spiritual truth	Unable to perceive spiritual truth
Unregenerate Will	Able to receive salvation only through Holy Spirit	Able to receive salvation only through Holy Spirit
Nature of Logic	Applies to all reality, finite and infinite	Applies only to finite reality; infinite reality is beyond logic
Apologetics and Evangelism	Sees a distinction	Sees no distinction
Purpose of Apologetics	To present evidence to the unbeliever and to persuade through logical evidence	To defend the Christian faith, while recognizing no common ground with the unbeliever
Value of Apologetics to Unbeliever	To give evidence and reasons for faith	None
Value of Apologetics to Believer	To confirm in the faith and render faith credible to unbeliever	To confirm in the faith

Chart 9

PART 2
PHILOSOPHICAL
APOLOGETICS

Using Philosophy in Apologetics

Reasons Against	Reasons For
Philosophy relies on esoteric assumptions without any basis in reality.	Certain assumptions are philosophically undeniable, such as the "real" laws of logic.
Philosophy cannot yield absolute certainty, it is only a speculative pursuit.	Most fields of study, including science, do not yield absolute certainty, yet we accept them as valid and beneficial disciplines. Philosophy does yield certainty in many areas, such as the nature of logic, truth, and self-existence, since to deny any of these would rationally be tantamount to affirming them.
Philosophy is not verifiable through observation or experience.	Nor is this objection verifiable even though the objection does have meaning and value to the one making the objection.
Philosophy in apologetics has no practical value. Nor does it promote one's godly character. What do you do with it?	This objection makes the mistake of assuming that if something is not usable in practical terms, then it is of no value. But there are many things the philosopher can "do": think clearly, evaluate literature to avoid deception, make wise decisions, teach, and be a better person as a result of thinking properly.
The apostle Paul warned the church when he said, "Beware lest anyone cheat you through philosophy and empty deceit" (Colossians 2:8).	Most likely Paul was speaking about a particular philosophy (probably an incipient gnosticism) since the Greek text shows the definite article (tas, the) directly preceding the word "philosophy." Paul is speaking of a negative kind of philosophy characterized by the "tradition of men," the "basic principles of the world," and "not according to Christ" (see Acts 17:28–29).
The discipline of philosophy has secular (Thales, Heraclitus, Socrates, Plato, Aristotle) and pagan origins (Oracle of Delphi) and should be avoided.	One who rejects truth or a discipline simply because of its origins commits the "Genetic Fallacy." If this objection is true, then many beneficial aspects of medicine, science, mathematics, education, and logic should be avoided (e.g., Philippians 4:8).
Empirical science offers a higher degree of certainty since it is visually based and can be repeatedly tested in order to confirm results.	Even empirical science has philosophical elements that cannot themselves be discovered or supported through use of the scientific method, such as knowledge, logic, morality, and being. To deny these nonempirical realities would be to undermine empirical science.
Philosophy elevates reason over the Bible and makes mankind instead of Scripture the test for truth.	Prior to salvation, reason must be used to evaluate the truthfulness of religious literature. After salvation, one's thinking must be in accord with, and submitted to, God's revelation in the Bible.

Chart 10

Types of Philosophy

	Speculative	Analytic/Conceptual
Goals	To explain the ultimate constituents of the world and reality. To define the proper place in this world of mankind and mankind's activities.	To examine basic presuppositions and concepts that those in the special disciplines use, i.e., the scientist, moralist, and theologian. To clarify the concepts and terms used in all major areas of inquiry. To analyze the foundations of knowledge.
Central Concern	To synthesize the results of conceptual inquiry into a comprehensive and integrated view of reality (e.g., metaphysics). To formulate a unified system of religious, moral, and aesthetic value.	To define philosophic and scientific terms and clarify the language used to express ideas.
Key Concepts	Employs the use of questions that ask for descriptive and prescriptive answers: What is ...? What ought to be ...?	Employs the verification principle which states, in essence, that for a statement to be meaningful there must be the ability to verify its truthfulness either by definition or by empirical means (known through the five senses). All other statements are meaningless.
History	Has a very long and noble history, starting in the 5th and 4th centuries BC with Socrates, Plato, and Aristotle.	In the early 12th century, it was recognized as a separate school within philosophy.
Objections	1. Integration of all knowledge and values is impossible. 2. Speculative questions cannot be decided based on mankind's experience.	1. The "search" for meaning is emphasized as coming to objective truth. 2. The verification principle is considered by many as an unreliable test of meaning or meaningfulness and may be self-destructive since the verification cannot itself be verified by its own criteria.
Proponents	Plato (c. 428–c. 347 BC) Plotinus (AD 205–270) G. W. F. Hegel (1770–1831) Thomas Aquinas (c. 1225–c. 1274)	George Edward Moore (1873–1958) Bertrand Russell (1872–1970) Ludwig Wittgenstein (1889–1951) A. J. Ayer (1910–1989)
Recommended Reading	Henry B. Veatch. *Two Logics: The Conflict Between Classical and Neo-Analytic Philosophy* (Evanston: Northwestern University Press, 1969).	

Chart 11

Philosophical Inquiry

Philosophical reasoning does not in itself solve theological debate, for it is ancillary to the disciplines of theology and apologetics. Its purpose is primarily that of methodology and clarification of principles (such as the existence of God, nature of truth, nature of reality). Since apologetics focuses on providing a defense of a Christian view of the world, philosophy assists the apologist by offering a rationale for acceptance of objective truth regarding the Bible, science, and other areas of apologetic concern. Why study philosophy? It causes us to carefully evaluate our presuppositions, prejudices, and arguments to discover if they correspond to reality and are consistent with biblical truth, thus contributing to the understanding of our faith and to greater appreciation of the God we worship.

Term	Definition/Example	Proponents' Arguments	Opponents' Arguments	Time
Philosophy	Greek root meaning "love of wisdom." —Plato and Aristotle. "The unexamined life isn't worth living." —Socrates	Philosophy is the "queen of sciences" general and universal, since no discipline functions without a philosophical foundation.	Philosophy is not a science at all, but a rational activity with no convincing arguments.	Origin: Miletus, with Thales, Greece 600 BC
Analytical or Conceptual Analysis	Popular in North America and Europe. This branch of philosophy analyzes the foundations of knowledge and how the world is. A study of concepts and terminology.	Analytical philosophy clarifies the terms used in an area of inquiry. This approach is known as "metaphilosophical," or the philosophy of philosophy.	Overemphasizes meaning of words and underemphasizes truth. Verification principle, which states that a statement is meaningful only if purely definitional or verifiable by one of the five senses, is unreliable and may be self-defeating.	Origin: Plato, *Gorgias* School of thought: 20th century
Speculative Philosophy	Synthesizes results of analytical inquiry into a comprehensive view of reality, which answers questions such as "What are the roles of education?" "What is the correct standard of morality?"	An attempt is made to integrate all knowledge into a single view of reality and a unified system of religious, moral, and aesthetic value.	The integration of all knowledge and values is impossible, requiring an infallible mind. This asks too much of philosophy and is nonsense, making this form of philosophy a pseudo-science, without subject matter.	History of this philosophy is long, but it has recently come into disfavor in North America and in Europe.

Chart 12

Tools of Philosophy

Argument	Any group of statements or propositions, one of which is claimed to follow from the others. These statements then provide the grounds for the conclusion. There are two distinct types of arguments: inductive and deductive, both of which are said to require either good evidence to support the truthfulness of the premises or the premises must be known to be true, which is an issue of certainty that addresses the truth-value of the premises themselves. The former, inductive argument, is known as a "reliable argument," and the latter, deductive argument, as a "conclusive argument."
Inductive Argument	The premises are claimed to give some evidence for the conclusion. At best, the conclusion can be stated as probably true.
Deductive Argument	If formed correctly, the premises in a deductive argument should guarantee the conclusion through logical necessity. To achieve this, the premises must follow certain central concepts: • *Validity*: Premises must be valid for the conclusion to be valid. It is possible for an invalid argument to have true premises and a false conclusion or a true conclusion and false premises. • *Soundness*: In real arguments, we are concerned with validity, but also soundness. A sound argument has true premises and a conclusion that follows.
Reliable Argument	A valid argument has good evidence that the premises are true. Of course, there are degrees of reliability.
Conclusive Argument	George Edward Moore said that it is not enough to have a sound argument; an argument must also be conclusive, with premises known to be true. It is questionable whether this form of argument exists.
Clarity	To determine whether a proposition is true, we must first understand its meaning. Two distinct forms of clarity are addressed: definition and analysis of concepts.
Definitions	Definitions put forth a statement of the necessary and sufficient conditions for the use of words. The two types of definitions are: • *Nominal*: An arbitrary stipulation that a certain word will have a certain meaning. Includes the use of words as symbols to have them mean whatever we need them to mean at the time. • *Real*: Description of the set of properties possessed by all members of a certain class and not possessed by anything outside of that class. These can be true or false. A nominative cannot be false for it is bound to whatever meaning it is given at that particular time and place and purpose.
Analysis of concepts	Analysis of concepts is a process of defining and clarifying terms.
A priori	The truth of a statement or proposition is self-evident prior to or independent of experience.

Chart 13

Tools of Philosophy (continued)

A posteriori	The truth of a statement or proposition is determined by appeal to factual evidence following from and tested by experience.

Deductive Syllogisms	The six rules to follow for valid deductive arguments are:
	   1. A valid categorical syllogism must contain only three terms, no term being used in an equivocal sense.
	   2. In a valid categorical syllogism, the middle term must be distributed at least once in the premises.
	   3. In a valid syllogism, no term can be distributed in the conclusion which is not also distributed in the premises.
	   4. No categorical syllogism is valid which has two negative premises.
	   5. If one premise of a categorical syllogism is negative, then the conclusion must be negative.
	   6. No valid categorical syllogism with a particular conclusion can have two universal premises.

Fallacies that occur when these rules are not followed	
1. Fallacy of **Four Terms** All valid categorical syllogisms have three terms that have consistent meaning throughout the argument. When there are more than three, the argument is no longer valid.	**Cows** are **brown**. **Animals** have **four legs**. Cows have four legs.
2. Fallacy of the **Undistributed Middle** Occurs when the middle term ("mammals," the term used in both premises) fails to connect the two other terms ("dogs," "monkeys") with each other. The premises show no relationship between dogs and monkeys. Therefore, the conclusion, that all dogs are monkeys, is invalid.	All dogs are **mammals**. All monkeys are **mammals**. All dogs are monkeys.
3. Fallacy of the **Illicit Major** Occurs when the major term ("mammals") is undistributed (not linked with both of the other two terms, "dogs" and "monkeys") and the conclusion makes an invalid assertion about the major term. The major premise ("all dogs are mammals") is limited to a particular group of mammals ("all dogs") and makes no reference to "monkeys.".	All dogs are **mammals**. No monkeys are dogs. No monkeys are mammals.
4. Fallacy of **Exclusive Premises** Occurs when a syllogism has two negative premises and falsely implies a relationship between the two (dogs and cats) in the conclusion. Both the major and minor premises deal with mutually exclusive classes.	**No dogs** are mammals. **No cats** are mammals. No dogs are cats.
5. **Existential** Fallacy Occurs when two *universal* premises (indicated by the words *all* or *no*) form a *particular* conclusion (indicated by the word *some*) by assuming facts not in evidence; the major and minor premises do not explicitly assert that there is a class of dogs and unicorns that actually exists.	**All dogs** are animals. **No unicorns** are animals. Some unicorns are not dogs.

Chart 13

Disciplines within Philosophy

Ethics	The term "ethics" refers both to a set of principles of right conduct and a discipline that studies those principles. Ethics, as a theoretical subject, denotes a branch of philosophy. It is distinguishable from other disciplines in philosophy because it is interested in what is correct and of ultimate worth in the good life. The purpose of ethical theorizing is an effort to solve practical and immediate problems.
Meta-Ethics	The search for the meaning of certain key terms that appear in ethical statements, such as "good," "wrong," "ought," and "should."
Normative Inquiry	The philosophical practice of considering ethical theories that recommend, appraise, and justify the choice of a certain action.
Moral or Ethical Relativism	A view that states that universal or absolute principles are impossible to attain, and that ethical rules are situational or culturally dependent. This view is defended by Joseph Fletcher in *Situation Ethics*.
Emotivism	Defended by A. J. Ayer and C. L. Stevenson, this process claims that statements of moral principle are not prescriptive, but express personal opinions of approval or disapproval.
Social and Political Philosophy	This philosophical thought falls into two distinct but interrelated classes. The first examines why society is the way it is. This thought can be ultimately classified in the disciplines of psychology, anthropology, political science, and economics. The second class examines the goals of society and what part the state plays in achieving those goals. "Who should govern society?" "What is the meaning of democracy and is it a justifiable form of government?" These are questions for a social and political philosopher.
Aesthetics	An essential part of the value theory, or axiology, aesthetics attempts to critically examine what is beautiful and ordered, such as art, music, and literature. "What makes a good poem, painting, symphony, etc.?"
Logic	A rational inquiry that sets forth systematic laws of thought and argument using deductive arguments with structured premises and conclusions (e.g., Matthew 22:41-46). A fallacy in logic exists when an argument is brought against a person without the facts or evidence involved. This type of attack is called *argumentum ad hominem* (argument against the man).
Deductive Logic or Syllogisms	A form of logical argument first set down by Aristotle (384–322 BC), consists of a major premise, a minor premise, and a conclusion. If the premises are true, a valid conclusion necessarily follows.
Symbolic Logic	A modified symbolic form of deductive Aristotelian logic, this form looks more like mathematical equations. The men most responsible for symbolic logic are Gottlob Frege (1848–1925), Bertrand Russell (1872–1970), and Alfred North Whitehead (1861–1947).
Modal Logic	Deals with three principal modes of philosophy: impossibility, contingency, and necessity. These modes are then interpreted in possible worlds. "Impossibility" means that a statement is false in every possible world. "Necessity" means that a statement is true in every possible world. "Contingency" means that a statement is true in at least one possible world.
Deontic	Related to ethics, attempts to put into formal structure the functioning of the words "ought" or "should" in moral contexts and statements.

Chart 14

Disciplines within Philosophy (continued)

Doxastic	Deals with statements that begin with "I think," "I believe." These statements affect the truth value of statements.
Philosophy of Religion	The analyzation and evaluation of the information of a certain religion gathered by historians and comparativists of that religion. The questions asked by the philosopher of religion are those dealing with the nature of the religion itself, its defining characteristics or core ideas. The philosopher also critically analyzes the existence of God (Immanuel Kant) and the attributes of God. The philosopher can tackle the more difficult questions of religion, such as its language and meaning (Thomas Aquinas) and the problem of evil.
History of Philosophy	Historical study of the influences that led to the formulation of ideas, the effect of those ideas, or the person who wrote them.
Philosophy of History/Science	The critical reflection about a discipline of study that exists in our world. Any discipline is open to such analysis. Philosophy is a second-order discipline, that is, it studies the thought and elements of an already existent discipline.
Epistemology	The investigation of the origin, nature, and the accumulation process of knowledge. The two major branches within epistemological debate are rationalism and empiricism.
Metaphysics	Literally meaning "after physics" in Greek. This thought process was named by Andronicus of Rhodes to designate the unnamed books that appeared after Aristotle's *Physics*. Through the use of the term "beyond" or "after," the term *metaphysics* has come to be known as beyond the physical, a study of being or reality. "What are the ultimate, objective constituents of reality?" "What is the nature of space and time?" "Must every event have a cause?"
Action Theory	The study of the relationship of mental states to actions. "What is an act, and how is it related to an agent?" "What is the connection between act and desire?"

Chart 14

Types of Certainty

Type	Proponent	Description	Objections	Defense
Moral Commands	Immanuel Kant (1724–1804)	Moral Absolutism: Moral statements contain the "ought" of duty. They are categorical and universal.	Ethical choices are arbitrary. Different cultures maintain different moral standards.	If moral choice is arbitrary, then any choice is equally permissible. Hitler's violent war crimes would be morally justifiable. Morality is not as diverse as some would claim. There is general agreement between cultures on items of intrinsic value (i.e., the value of life).
Knowledge of the External World	René Descartes (1596–1650)	Existence of the outside world is the cause of one's perception.	David Hume: Perception, and therefore certainty, is the product of one's mind. Knowledge cannot be certain, only probable.	Hume's objection fails to pass his own test of certainty and is therefore unsuccessful.
	G. E. Moore (1873–1958)	To experience the physical is to know that it is real. "Here is my right hand, and here is my left."		
Self-Awareness	René Descartes (1596–1650)	"I think, therefore I am." Mental exercise is proof of personal existence.	Gilbert Ryle: 1. We can never give a complete description of ourselves. 2. The object or thing, which we label "I," is only a phantom.	Ryle's argument is invalid. He cannot prove the non-existence of self, but merely that self is difficult or impossible to completely describe.
Logical and Mathematical Knowledge	Plato (c. 428–c. 347 BC)	The recognition of a fixed system which can be calculated and/or logically deduced.	This type of certainty does not pertain to the real world, but only to the possibility of a hypothetical system. John Stuart Mill: The laws of logic are empirical generalizations open to correction. Another set of laws, though presently inconceivable, may be possible.	Logical and mathematical laws are neither merely general nor only possible, but specifically verifiable and actual.

Chart 15

Kinds of Philosophical Certainty

Kind	Proponent	Description
Apodictic	René Descartes (1596–1650)	A necessary or absolute truth which is impervious to doubt. Indubitability—the exclusion of all doubt. Incorrigibility—incapable of being corrected.
Psychological	David Hume (1711–1776)	Certainty is grounded in the knower, rather than the object. The knower is certain because he has no reason to doubt. The weight of truth rests on the belief of the knower and not on the thing known.
Pragmatic	Clarence I. Lewis (1883–1964)	Certainty based on convenience. An object or statement is true if it benefits present experience. Truth is relative to the experience with which it is associated.
Probability	John Locke (1632–1704)	A statement is accepted on the basis of the strength of evidence which supports it even though certainty is impossible.

Chart 16

Methodology in Philosophy

The presentation of Old World and New World indicates two major movements in methodology used in philosophy, not a history of philosophy. The methodology used until the scientific era began reflected that which was established by philosophers such as Socrates, Plato, Zeno, and Aristotle. In the 16th century, a new methodology began which was particularly influenced by the work of Bacon, Descartes, and Mill.

Old World (Premodern, prior to 1500s)

Socrates (469–399 BC) Plato (c. 428–c. 347 BC)	Induction method of philosophy. Socrates used the question-and-answer method of philosophical pursuit. His belief was that all men had truth inborn, for they knew truth from a previous existence. To Socrates, philosophy was but a "midwife" that gave birth to the ideas within one's own mind when that mind was properly "jogged" to recall.
Zeno (c. 490–c. 425 BC)	Pupil of Parmenides, Zeno developed the method of *Reductio ad Absurdum*, or the reduction of alternative positions to the point of absurdity. This is a valuable tool because any view that generates contradictions cannot be true (the Law of Non-Contradiction).
Aristotle (384–322 BC)	Widely held as the originator of deductive logic, which argues from the general to the particular, with a major and minor premise and a conclusion. The series of propositions is called a "syllogism." Deductive logic relies on universally true premises, which are hard to find.

New World (Modern, 1500s until today)

Francis Bacon (1561–1626)	Credited with the overthrow of the "old" deductive method with the "new" inductive method, Bacon urged men to cease being scholastic "spiders" that spin truth out of their own deductive reasoning and become scientific "bees" who transform nature's nectar of truth into practical products that can benefit mankind. He formulated the rules for induction in *Novum Organum*, 2.XI. This became the forerunner for *Canons of Inductive Logic* by John Stuart Mill.	
	Deductive All men are mortal. Socrates is a man. Socrates is mortal.	*Inductive* All observable elements of a wall are stone. The whole wall is stone.

René Descartes (1596–1650)	Descartes is credited with establishing methodological doubt as a method to discover certainty. His distrust in empiricism (knowledge based on observations using the five senses) led him to pure rationalism. His rationalistic methodology is best represented by his minimalistic dictum *ergo cogito sum* (I think therefore I am), in contrast to an empirical perspective of *ergo sum cogito* (I am therefore I think).

John Stuart Mill (1806–1873)	Mills' inductive method as put forth in *Canons of Inductive Logic* can be summarized by four rules:
	    The Method of Agreement: The one factor common to all situations that precede where an effect occurs is probably the cause of the effect.
	    The Method of Difference: Whenever an effect occurs when A is present but not when it is absent, then A is probably the cause of the effect.
	    The Joint Method: Combine the first two methods when one method alone does not yield a definite result.
	    The Method of Concomitant Variations: When a factor precedes an effect to a similar degree as the effect, this factor is probably the cause of the effect.

Scientific Method	Neither entirely inductive nor deductive, the scientific method is generally viewed as being composed of several elements:
	  • Observation of phenomenon or phenomena.
	  • Formulation of a hypothesis that explains the phenomenon.
	  • Attempt to use the hypothesis to predict other phenomena or quantify the results of new observations.
	  • Tests of the hypothesis by independent experimenters under controlled conditions.
	  • If the experiments and results are consistent, then the hypothesis may become a theory or law.
	Adapted from Frank Wolfs, University of Rochester, "Introduction to the Scientific Method," *http://teacher.nsrl.rochester.edu/phy_labs/AppendixE/AppendixE.html*.

Chart 17

Methodology in Philosophy (continued)

Søren Kierkegaard (1813–1855)	In clear reaction against the scientific method, Kierkegaard developed the existential method of philosophy. While not denying that objective scientific truth exists, he did not consider that to be the most important form of truth. In his method, there was nothing as important as subjective truth. Unless one believes something subjectively and passionately, he does not possess the truth. Only by an act of will, or "leap of faith," does one place oneself in truth. In *Fear and Trembling*, he shows how Abraham, when up on the hill with Isaac, must shed his objective, rational realm and transcend into a more personal religious realm.
Edmund Husserl (1859–1938)	Founder of the phenomenological method of philosophy, an attempt to get back to a pre-theoretical approach to one's primary awarenesses. It attempts to be without presuppositions—letting the bare facts of one's primary experience "speak for themselves." Through phenomenological reduction, Husserl attempts to avoid presuppositions by deferring all questions of existence. This philosophy is valuable in that it affirms that subjectivity is not to be excluded from the realm of truth.
Martin Heidegger (1889–1967)	Borrowed Husserl's method and applied it to the study of man. He concluded that man is a being-in-time or a being-unto-death, thrust into the world and headed for death with no explanation. Man as a being-unto-nothingness, then, is the fundamental structure of reality of the phenomenological method.
Jean-Paul Sartre (1905–1980)	Man is a "useless passion" and all of life is an empty bubble on a sea of nothingness. High existential despair such as this is usually the conclusion arrived at by the phenomenological method.
Analytical Method	Has two methodologies, verification and clarification. *Verification*: A. J. Ayer, Moritz Schlick, and Rudolf Carnap were the men of the Vienna Circle of the 1920s who began the logical positivism movement in general. The verification method arose from the verification principle put forth in Ayer's *Language, Truth and Logic*, which stated that for a statement to be meaningful, it must be either purely definitional or verifiable by one or more of the five senses. The negative side to this principle, called the "falsification principle" put forth by Antony Flew (1923–), states that any statement or proposition is meaningless unless it is subject to falsification. If you won't allow anything to count against your statement, then nothing should count for it. *Clarification*: This comes directly from Ludwig Wittgenstein, who believed that philosophical puzzles in the pursuit of truth could be solved by analysis (clarification) of language. Ambiguity leads to confusion.

Chart 17

Laws of Logic and Objections

Laws of Logic

Law	Definition	Form	Symbolic Form	Example
The Law of Identity	A statement or proposition is identical to itself. (John 6:35)	A is A	$p = p$	Socrates is Socrates.
The Law of Excluded Middle	Every statement is either true or false, with no middle alternative. (Matthew 12:30; 22:41–46)	A is either A or non-A	$p \lor \sim p$	Socrates is either Socrates or not Socrates.
The Law of Non-Contradiction	No statement can be both true and false at the same time and in the same sense. (1 Timothy 6:20)	A is not non-A	$p \neq \sim p$	Socrates cannot be Socrates and not Socrates.
The Law of Rational Inference	Inferences can be made by reasoning from a series of premises to a conclusion. (1 Corinthians 15:12–19)	A is in B, B is in C, therefore, A is in C		Socrates is in the room, the room is in the house, therefore, Socrates is in the house.

Objections to Logic

Objection	Response
There are no laws of logic that are absolutely certain.	The laws of logic are undeniable and self-evident. When attempting to deny them one actually affirms them. For example, the statement "There are no laws of logic" assumes the very principles the statement seeks to deny, namely, it employs laws of logic to make the distinction between the existence and non-existence of laws of logic.
Logic is only man's reasoning and does not apply to God.	This objection is self-defeating since it utilizes "man's reasoning" and is a logical statement about God. Either the objection is logical or it is not. If it is logical, then the objection defeats itself. If the objection is not logical, then it is illogical, with no reason for anyone to believe the objection is true.
Using logic makes God subject to human logic.	This objection confuses the source of logic. Logic flows from the nature of God, not from humans. God determined logic; humans only discovered it. Theology and apologetics do not scrutinize God with logic. Only our statements about God are evaluated with logic. Since logic comes from God, we are not testing our statements about God by a standard outside of Himself.
God can and often does work against logic (Isaiah 55:8–9) and human wisdom (1 Corinthians 1:19–2:16).	God may—and indeed does—often act and think beyond the human ability to understand, but never contrary to local laws (Isaiah 1:18; Philippians 4:8; Romans 12:1–3; 1 Timothy 6:20). The objection fails to make the distinction between human wisdom that is "of this world" and godly wisdom that derives its source from heaven (1 Corinthians 1:20–21; Proverbs 1:7; 8:10–11).

Chart 18

Laws of Logic and Objections (continued)

God violates the laws of nature through miracles; he therefore can violate the laws of logic.	Although God does break or suspend the laws of nature on occasion through miraculous acts, natural laws are of a different kind from the laws of logic. Natural laws are descriptive and, as such, only describe the way nature operates, not how it must operate. Laws of logic are prescriptive, directing the way people should think, not how they do think.
If God can do the impossible (Matthew 19:26; Luke 1:37), he can break the laws of logic.	It is true that God can do the "impossible" if one is speaking of doing what is humanly impossible. But God cannot do what is actually impossible, such as creating a triangular square, lying (Numbers 23:19; Hebrews 6:18), changing (Malachi 3:6), or denying himself (2 Timothy 2:13).
Logic cannot save anyone, so why bother using it?	The purpose of logic is not salvific, though thinking logically may cause one to perceive better the claims of the gospel. Much that is truth is not directly related to the fact of redemption, but is important for living and thinking correctly about God and His truth. Logic, knowledge, or wisdom cannot save anyone. Neither can moral conduct, since it is only through faith that a spiritual rebirth takes place (John 3; Ephesians 2:8–9; Titus 3:5). But does this mean people should abolish moral living? No.
People do not always think logically, so why bother utilizing logic?	Since people do not always act morally, should we give up living a moral lifestyle? No.

Adapted from Norman L. Geisler and Ronald M. Brooks, *Come Let Us Reason* (Grand Rapids: Baker, 1990), 17–20.

Chart 18

Informal Fallacies

"Informal fallacy" is a broad category of fallacies that result from a mistake that occurs within the content or reasoning of an argument due to carelessness, ambiguity, or irrelevance, in contrast to the category "formal fallacy," which is a broad category of fallacies that result from the improper structure or form of an argument.

Fallacy	Explanation
Accent	Ambiguity of argument that results from improper tone of voice and emphasis of a given proposition
Ambiguity	Various informal fallacies that make communication unclear or ambiguous
Ab Annis	Appeal to age as determinative of truth
Ad Baculum	Appeal to force or fear as determinative of truth
Ad Futuris	Appeal to future possibilities as determinative of truth
Ad Hominem	Appeal to the person (abusive or circumstantial) as determinative of truth
Ad Ignorantiam	Appeal to one's lack of knowledge or proof concerning an issue as determinative of truth
Ad Misericordiam	Appeal to pity or misery of an individual as determinative of truth
Ad Populum	Appeal to what is popular or in vogue as determinative of truth
Ad Verecundiam	Appeal to an inappropriate authority as determinative of truth
Amphibole	Appeal to ambiguous propositions that cloud the meaning of a truth statement due to awkward wording
Analogy	An attempt to use similarity that is irrelevant to the argument
Argument of the Beard	Appealing to imperceptible differences among extremes to indicate there are no real differences among them
Category Mistake	Confusing things in one category with things from another category: "What does the color red taste like?"
Composition	Assuming that what is true of the parts is equally true of the whole
Dicto Simpliciter	Attempting to apply a general rule to a specific case when differences exist that militate against its application
Division	Assuming that what is true of a whole is also true of its parts
Equivocation	Change in the meaning of a word in the midst of an argument though the overall context remains the same; "Some horses have short tails. My horse has a short tail. Therefore, my horse is *some* horse."

Chart 19

Informal Fallacies (continued)

Formal Fallacy	Broad category of fallacies that result from the improper structure or form of an argument
False Cause	Assigning what is not the cause of a given effect as its real cause, as in crediting one event as the cause of another event simply because the first occurs prior to the second. "The rooster causes the sun to rise." "Mosquitoes are the cause of malaria."
False Dilemma	Occurring when one is given only two alternatives to choose from when in fact there are at least one or more additional alternatives. "Either we allow abortion or we force children to be raised by parents who do not want them."
Hasty Generalization	Reaching a conclusion after analyzing only unusual cases instead of reasoning from analysis of typical cases
Non Sequitur	Occurring when the conclusion does not follow from the premises
Petitio Principii	Assuming in the premises of an argument the conclusion of what the argument is trying to prove (begging the question)
Relevance	Incorporating irrelevant material into an argument
Slippery Slope	Occurring when an individual claims that accepting a conclusion of an argument will lead to a series of undesirable consequences and justifications. "If high school students are allowed to decide which schools they want to attend, it will lead to a breakdown of discipline within the home, and ultimately lead to a rise in the juvenile crime rate and therefore, a lowered school attendance rate."
Straw Man	Occurring when one interprets an opposing or alternative viewpoint in its weakest form or inaccurately and then refutes it as if the strengths of the position are being addressed

Chart 19

Nature of Truth

Theories	Explanation	Criticism	Response	Proponents
Coherence Theory	Truth is defined in terms of internal propositional consistency. All statements within a system must be logically consistent with other statements in that same system for the conclusion to be true. If the system is logically connected and is consistent within itself and occupies a proper relationship with other judgments in that system, then it is true. If it does not, it is false.	Coherence theory lacks any external referent by which to test the statements within a given system. One may construct any system, including a mythical one, which perfectly measures up to other statements within the system, making such a mythical system true. But it is contradictory to consider a mythical system to be true. Many liken the coherence theory to building a house without any foundation. Internal consistency may reveal which system cannot be true, but cannot demonstrate which system is true.	The law of noncontradiction shows that a statement must be consistent within a system for it to remain within the possibility of truth. Something cannot be true if it is not consistent with any other statements in the system since it would then be considered contradictory. One should not dismiss an entire system because a nonessential statement contradicts another tenet. There is a difference between a true system with pockets of error and a false system with pockets of truth. Truth must necessarily be logically consistent, and whatever is not is necessarily false.	Benedict Spinoza G. W. F. Hegel Bradley and Bland Blanchard
Pragmatic Theory	Truth is understood in terms of expediency, actions, experience, practice, results, or by what works. If true assumptions lead to actions that have utility or bring beneficial results, they are considered true.	If truth is defined by what works, it would be difficult to discover what is true since identical ideas, concepts, and propositions that contain truth value yield differing conclusions for different people. Truth can "work" and bring intended results, but occasionally unintended results are the end product, as when parents feed, nurture, and love their children, but the children become tyrants. Someone may lie to gain some benefit, but that doesn't make their lie true since a true lie would be a contradiction. Some suggest that function and utility are not in the same category as a truth statement regarding an item. Function describes what something does, not what it is.	Without something practical or concrete by which to discover the truth value of our beliefs, we appear left in subjectivism. Even the much acclaimed scientific method seeks general truth through results and experience. It would appear to go against logic to reject as true the vital benefits that are accorded to an individual through belief in some things, such as God, that cannot be verified through use of the five senses.	Charles Sanders Peirce John Dewey William James

Chart 20

			Aristotle Bertrand Russell Alfred Tarski
Intentional/ Subjective Theory	Truth is defined in terms of emotions, feelings, sincerity, or intentions. Statements and affirmations do not contain truth value as in objectivism; instead, truth is rooted within the subjective characteristics of an individual.	A truth statement must correspond to its referent in the real world or the statement possesses no more value than one's own mere opinion. If this is the case, there can be no objective truth. However, this conclusion must be false since to say, "There is no objective truth" is self-defeating and represents an objective truth. Truth is not found in what one doesn't say but in what one does say. Feelings change from day to day, but if this is true, then subjective truth changes also and will ultimately lead to a breakdown of communication and moral behavior. If truth is subjective, no one could verify its validity, since the basis for truth is located inside the individual consciousness.	Truth cannot be relegated to mere facts in the real world since many statements about things we universally know to be true cannot be verified extra-mentally (e.g., numbers, logic). Truth is often personal and cannot be divorced from the individual determining it. To do so would dismiss and subvert the vital element (subjectivism) and its relationship to truth.
Correspondence Theory	Truth can be defined as those statements, propositions, affirmations, and judgments that correctly correspond to its extra-mental referent in the real world as it exists. Truth value is contained in indicative statements about reality regardless of what anyone else thinks or feels about the matter. Statements that accurately reflect the current state of affairs are true, and those propositions that do not accurately correspond to reality are false.	Though the correspondence theory can be applied to some statements, it cannot be applied universally. For to say that "God exists" is true only if it corresponds to a referent outside of God would make the referent superior to God since He must conform to another. Some statements that refer to singular events, such as the beginning of first life, have no verifiable referent and cannot be considered true as tested by the correspondence theory's own criteria.	There must be some kind of correspondence between our statements and the real world or verifiable objective truth would be impossible. The statement "truth does not correspond to the way things actually are" purports to correspond to reality and therefore is self-defeating. God needs only to perfectly correspond to Himself as His ideas correspond to His being. Ultimately God is the referent to which all else must correspond. The verification of past events does not rule out the correspondence view of truth, since there could be eyewitnesses to the event, or one could give the benefit of the doubt to those things and events that cannot be verified if other such related statements are found to be true. Whether one can verify a statement has no bearing on the truthfulness of the statement, since there are certain judgments most believe to be true apart from any verification. If one cannot positively verify a cause of first life, that does not mean it is not true that there was a cause of first life.

Adapted from Norman L. Geisler, *Baker's Encyclopedia of Christian Apologetics* (Grand Rapids: Baker, 1999), 741–45.

Chart 20

How Can Truth Be Known?

Way of Knowing	Explanation	Philosophers
Correspondence	Truth is what corresponds to reality and is known through objective means.	Aristotle, 4th century BC Bertrand Russell, 19th–20th centuries Alfred Tarski, 20th century
Relativism	Denial that there are universal truths that apply to all people, in all places, and at all times, regardless of the knower's awareness or philosophical or religious perspective. The relativist usually appeals to personal perspective, power, situation, and autonomy rather than an objective foundation as the basis for truth, values, and meaning.	Protagoras, 5th century BC Thrasymachus, 5th century BC Joseph Fletcher, 20th century

Subjectivism	Knower has some kind of direct contact with object of belief. Knows object through experience or reason.
	    Rational Subjectivism: direct or common-sense
	      phenomenology (Husserl)
	    Suprarational Subjectivism: mysticism crisis or
	      encounter theology (Buber)
	    Existentialism: truth is determined by one's own
	      encounter with the world by an act of choice
	      (Sartre)
		Edmund Husserl, 19th–20th centuries
		Martin Buber, 19th–20th centuries
		Jean-Paul Sartre, 20th century

Rationalism	Look to reason instead of empirical data for origin and justification of beliefs.	René Descartes, 17th century Benedictus de Spinoza, 17th century Gottfried Leibniz, 17th–18th centuries
Empiricism	Source of knowledge comes from experience of one or more of the five senses.	John Locke, 17th century David Hume, 18th century George Berkeley, 17th–18th centuries
Pragmatism	Belief that if something works, has utility, or accomplishes something, it is true and certain.	William James, 19th–20th centuries John Dewey, 19th–20th centuries Charles Sanders Peirce, 19th–20th centuries

Chart 21

Tests for Truth

Test	Explanation	Purpose
Internal Consistency	Statement must be consistent with itself and other statements in a given system.	Negative test[1] that reveals what cannot possibly be true.
External Consistency	Truth claims must be consistent with confirmed truths previously known to all fields of study.	Negative test that reveals what cannot possibly be true.
Correspondence	Truth is discovered through corresponding statements, affirmations, and propositions to reality as it exists.	Positive test that identifies what is absolutely true.
Practical Benefit	Investigates the logical and practical conclusions of adopting a particular truth claim. If the statement or system yields no practical value, it may be false.	Test that seeks to discover the practical benefits, whether constructive or destructive, as the truth claim pertains to life and conduct.
Comprehensive Extent	Truth must be all-extensive and able to answer and stand against difficult questions and issues within its category as well as remain consistent with other known universal truths.	Negative test which seeks to discover the soundness of a truth claim as it extends universally to a broad category of issues.
Authority	Attempt to understand the credentials, reputation, character, motivation, and bias of eyewitnesses that serve as authoritative sources supporting a truth claim in an effort to discover their credibility.	A circumstantial test in which emphasis is placed on discovering the qualifications, personal nature, and motivating factors associated with an authority for a particular truth claim.

[1] "Negative test" is a limited kind of scrutiny that can reveal why a truth claim cannot possibly be true without simultaneously affirming the truth of the same claim.

Chart 22

Forms of Skepticism

Kinds	Explanation	Philosophers
Thoroughgoing or Complete	We have no knowledge beyond the knowledge of our own empirical experience.	Sextus Empiricus (2nd–3rd centuries) David Hume (18th century)
Mitigated	Knower has some kind of direct contact with object of belief. Knows object through experience or reason. a. *Rational Subjectivism*: direct or common-sense phenomenology (Husserl) b. *Suprarational Subjectivism*: mysticism crisis or encounter theology	Bishop John Wilkins (17th century) Joseph Glanvill (17th century) Immanuel Kant (18th century)
Limited	Particular types of knowledge claims are questioned. Any statement for which we cannot state the conditions that would count for or against its truth (falsifiability) cannot be knowledge (metaphysics).	A. J. Ayer (20th century) Antony Flew[1] (20th century)
Methodological or Cartesian	Arrival at indubitable knowledge through application of doubt to beliefs.	René Descartes (17th century)
Non-rationalism	No rational way to explain the world. No meaning or knowledge that is objectively true.	Many existentialists, including: Albert Camus (20th century) Leon Shestov (19th–20th centuries) Friedrich Nietzsche (19th century) Jean-Paul Sartre (20th century)

[1] Antony Flew in 2004 announced that he had rejected atheism and adopted a form of deism, but his position as a skeptic is still accurate. See interview in Winter 2005 issue of *Philosophia Christi*, the journal of the Evangelical Philosophical Society.

Chart 23

Views of Perception

	Perspective	Explanation	Objections	Defense	Proponents
Realism	Extreme or Primitive	Every experienced object exists independent of the observer. Perceptions are governed totally by the external world without alteration by the perceiver.	1. Universally understood that perceptions are, at times, misleading. 2. Has no way to account for illusory or hallucinated objects. 3. Does not consider the dependence that perception has on visual context (conditions alter perception).	1. Misleading perceptions are usually due to some fault of the perceiver, which does not alter the independence of the object. 2. Hallucinations or illusory objects are rare and of no consequence. 3. Experience of an object over time confirms its external reality.	Common Man
	Common Sense	Physical objects exist independent of the mind, but are directly observable to the mind. Perception is subjective, occurring exclusively in the mind. The mind "interprets" the objects.	1. Does not account for perceptions of physical objects that are misleading. 2. Does not consider variations of visual context.	This view accounts for illusory or hallucinated objects. Such perceptions are considered the product of the mind.	Thomas Reid (1710–1796) G. E. Moore (1873–1958)
Dualism	Representative Perception	"The Copy Theory" There are two distinct orders of existence: 1. Ideas: sense data which are immediate objects of perception. 2. Independent external world: the cause of sense data perceived by one's consciousness.	1. Is not an empirical theory, capable of proof or disproof. 2. Tends to lead to skepticism.	1. Accounts for illusion and error. 2. Handles perceptual relativity. 3. Distinguishes between primary and secondary qualities.	René Descartes (1596–1650)
	Phenomenalism	This describes the external world in "sense data" language rather than "material object" language. Speaks of what "seems to be," rather than what "is."	1. Is not an empirical theory, capable of proof or disproof. 2. Avoids the question of reality.	1. One cannot be wrong about what "appears" to be. 2. Does not assert or deny the possibility of a real external world. 3. The truth of a sense data statement does not depend on the actual existence of an object.	A. J. Ayer (1910–1989)

Chart 24

Idealism

	Description	Objections		Proponent
Weaker Form	Material objects cannot exist independently of some consciousness of them: "To be is to be perceived." *Physical perceptions* are caused by something beyond us and are universal. God is the source of physical perceptions of a material world. *Psychical perceptions* exist in and are caused by our minds.	1. God's proposed illusion of a material world would cast doubt on His integrity. To make an independent world appear to exist when it does not is deliberately misleading. 2. Goes against the natural tendency to accept a material object as the source of perception. 3. Impractical for everyday life.	1. There are only two things that exist: God and souls. All that our observation and experience can inform us is that we have ideas. 2. It is a mistake to assume that there exists anything besides ideas and those souls doing the perceiving.	Bishop George Berkeley (1685–1753)
Stronger Form	This adds to the above by positing certain categories of the mind, such as space, time, distance, and substance, that serve as necessary ingredients to conform the object of knowledge (e.g., tree, car) to the mind that knows it. This is a departure from the traditionally held view that says the human mind is conformed to the object known. That is to say, the mind shapes reality (i.e., objects of knowledge) instead of reality shaping the mind.	1. The view divorces reality from the realm of knowledge since it is the knower who provides/shapes the *content* of knowledge instead of the object of knowledge shaping the knower's mind to how and in what manner the object actually exists. 2. This view lacks a mechanism by which to hold the categories of the mind accountable. 3. Radical relativism results from the knowing process, since each knower can perceive an object differently. Therefore, knowledge that is unique, or even confined, to the knower cannot be objectively verified.	One cannot know appearances beyond this spacio-temporal world since the categories of the mind are structured to conform to only objects of knowledge gained from experience. Any attempt to violate this structure will result in contradictions known as "antinomies."	Immanuel Kant (1724–1804)

Chart 24

Views of Reality

View	Proponent	Argument	Objections
Monism: Reality Is One	Parmenides (c. 510–c. 450 BC)	1. Reality is either one or many. 2. If reality is many, then the many things must differ from each other. 3. There are only two ways things can differ: either by being (something) or by non-being (nothing). 4. Two things cannot differ by nothing. 5. Neither can things differ by something or being, because being is the only thing that everything has in common, and things cannot differ in the very respect in which they are the same. 6. Therefore, things cannot differ at all; everything is one.	1. Some argue that Parmenides' fourth statement is invalid because things can differ by "non-being." 2. Others assert that the fifth statement is inaccurate because things can differ in "being." 3. Parmenides' argument breaks down in that he does not justify his statements. They beg the question of truth.
	Zeno of Elea (c. 490–c. 425 BC)	1. If we assume reality is many, then absurd or impossible consequences follow. 2. Absurdity is a sign of falsity. 3. Therefore, it is false that reality is many. 4. Hence, reality must be one.	1. One need not assume that all reality is mathematically divisible. 2. Zeno's argument breaks down in the lack of justification for his statements. Why must one assume that absurd or impossible consequences result from the idea that reality is many?
Modified Monism	Plotinus (AD 205–270)	Unity is more ultimate than being. Pantheistic: from the One flows all multiplicity. Mind is the most unified. Matter is the most multiple and evil. Being differs by degree of unity.	1. Plotinus does not answer the problem. 2. Plotinus's "One" must have reality status. If being is that which is real, then the One is not actually beyond being, it is associated with it. 3. Being is not quantified, therefore it cannot differ by unity. Thus, the One is either completely real or is not real at all.

Chart 25

Pluralism: Reality Is Many	Leucippus (5th century BC) Democritus (c. 450–c. 370 BC)	Things differ by absolute non-being. Atoms differ in "space." Each atom occupies a different space in a void.	1. Does not answer Parmenides' challenge that differing by absolutely nothing is not differing at all. 2. Space is thought of as a relationship rather than a container.
	Plato (c. 428–c. 348 BC)	Things differ by relative non-being. All determination is by negation. An object is what it is because it is not everything else.[1]	1. Does not prove that differing by non-being is a real difference. 2. It is impossible to determine all things by negation.
	Aristotle (384–322 BC)	Ultimate items in the universe are "unmoved movers" (gods). Each god is a simple being in itself, yet different from the others in being.[2]	1. Does not answer Parmenides' question of how objects can or cannot differ in being. 2. In a universe with multiple gods, there would be no unity.
	Thomas Aquinas (c. 1225–c. 1274)	Being is not "entirely the same thing," but rather analogous (similar), since there are different kinds of being. Some have finite being (creation/man) and another has infinite being (God). Being is differentiated by its potential (i.e., what it can be). God is pure actuality which has no potential associated with His being (no ability to change, gain, or lose), however, man has potential. Finite being is differentiated from other finite being by the kind of potential associated with it. For example, a squirrel has differing potential from that of a human being. Only one thing is Being (God); everything else has being with diverse potentials. As finite immaterial beings, spirits are also composed of actuality and potentiality differing from other spirits by their diverse potentials.	1. A being with no potentiality (God) or ability to change is not capable of relating to act/potency (changing creation, man) being. This kind of being is considered "static" and not "dynamic." 2. Purely actual being with no potential (God) cannot create changing being (act/potency) since this implies a *change* of relationship between the creator (actuality) and creation (actuality/potentiality). However, this new relationship (change) implies potentiality in being that is supposed to be purely actual, which is a contradiction.
Flux: Reality Is Changing	Heraclitus (c. 536–475 BC)	Unlike Parmenides, reality is unified in a constant state of flux, alternating between opposites such as day and night, light and dark, hot and cold, and living and dying. These unending changes led to viewing the basic constituent of reality, both symbolically (as intellect) and literally (as descriptive of the transforming processes of nature), as *fire*. Although reality is in flux and change is inevitable, it all corresponds to the unchanging rational formula of unity known as the *logos*.	1. In a world of constant flux, knowledge is impossible since it does not allow a fixed point to which the spoken or written word may correspond. 2. Communication about reality would be subjective without a fixed point of reference. 3. In all changing things there must be something unchanging in order to measure progress/change.

1 This cell is adapted from Norman L. Geisler and Paul D. Feinberg, *Introduction to Philosophy: A Christian Perspective* (Grand Rapids: Baker, 1980), 171.

2 Ibid.

Chart 25

PART 3
THEISTIC
APOLOGETICS

Seven Major Worldviews

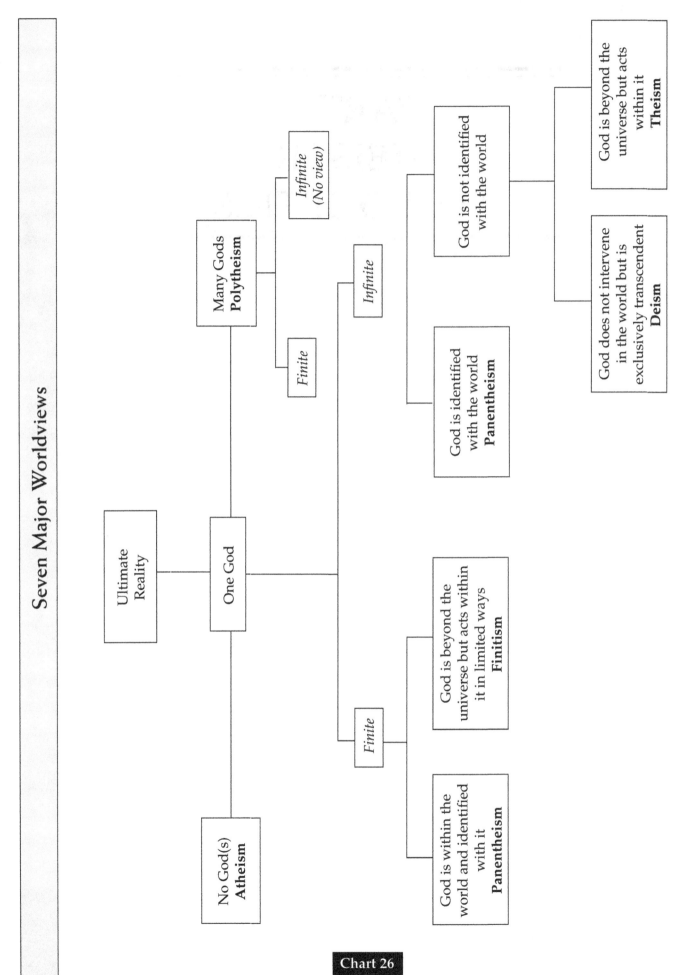

Ultimate Reality

- No God(s) **Atheism**
- One God
  - Finite
    - God is within the world and identified with it **Panentheism**
    - God is beyond the universe but acts within it in limited ways **Finitism**
  - Infinite
    - God is identified with the world **Panentheism**
    - God is not identified with the world
      - God does not intervene in the world but is exclusively transcendent **Deism**
      - God is beyond the universe but acts within it **Theism**
- Many Gods **Polytheism**
  - Finite
  - Infinite (*No view*)

Chart 26

Worldviews Contrasted

	Atheism	Deism	Theism	Finitism	Panentheism	Pantheism	Polytheism
God	No God	One God (Unitarian)	One God (Unitarian or Trinitarian)	One Limited God	One God in Process	One Impersonal God	More Than One God
Nature of God	No nature No metaphysical reality Has never existed nor will ever exist Arguments for God are either fallacious or unprovable	Eternal Infinite Impersonal Simple Unchangeable Pure Being with no potential to be anything else Eternal creator of the universe who alone possesses all the omnipredicates Now passive, no longer supernaturally active in world	Eternal Simple Unchangeable Pure Being with no potential to be anything else	Temporal Complex Changeable Personal but limited in power Cannot guarantee final victory over evil, therefore, God works (struggles) to bring about His will in the universe	Eternal Temporal Finite personal deity Dipolar: infinite pole and finite pole; both poles are changeable Infinite pole, unlimited in potential, distinct from world Finite pole is what is actual being identified with world Mutual dependency between the world and God	Eternal Impersonal Infinite Immanent, with no distinction between Himself and the world Simple Unchangeable Pure Being with no potential to be anything else	Temporal Complex Changeable Many finite personal gods/goddesses interact with world, limited in power, usually govern one aspect of reality (nature, love, war, etc.)
Origin of the Universe	Uncreated matter	*Ex nihilo* spirit/matter	*Ex nihilo* spirit/matter	*Ex materia or ex nihilo* spirit/matter	*Ex deo* spirit/matter	*Ex deo* spirit	*Ex materia* spirit/matter
Duration of Universe	Eternal	Finite Temporal	Finite Temporal	Eternal	Eternal	Eternal	Eternal
God's Relationship to Universe	None	Transcendent Transpersonal	Transcendent Immanent	Transcendent Immanent Personal Cannot guarantee victory over evil Struggles to bring about His will	Transcendent Personal Immanent Dependent on world, but world also dependent on God	No Transcendence Immanent Identical to world	Immanent
Miracles	No	Only one (creation)	Yes	Possible	No	No	Yes
Truth and Morality	Relative	Absolute	Absolute	Relative	Relative	Relative	Relative
Human Problem	Lack of education	Sin/rebellion cause separation from God	Sin/rebellion cause separation from God	Misuse of freedom and dependence on a limited God	Not following the direction and creativity of God	Ignorance of the divine self	Failure to satisfy/appease the gods
View of Jesus	Only a man	Only a man	God and man	Only a man	Only a man	Guru or divine manifestation	One of many gods

Chart 27

Worldviews Contrasted (continued)

	None / Annihilation	Soul survives / Reward or punish	Soul survives / Resurrection of the body	Soul survives / Reward or punish	Live as a memory in God	Reincarnation into another mortal body	Soul survives / Reward or punish
Life after Death	None Annihilation	Soul survives Reward or punish	Soul survives Resurrection of the body	Soul survives Reward or punish	Live as a memory in God	Reincarnation into another mortal body	Soul survives Reward or punish
Religious Association	Secular humanism	Some forms of liberal Christianity	Judaism Christianity Islam	None	None, maybe liberal Christianity	Hinduism Buddhism New Age Mind-science movements	Ancient nature religions Mormonism Hinduism Witchcraft Early Greeks and Romans
Evil	Real	Real	Real	Real	Real	Illusion	Real
Scriptural Contrast	It is foolish to be an atheist (Psalm 14:1). The Bible assumes the existence of God (Genesis 1:1).	God is immanent (2 Chronicles 16:9; Haggai 2:5; Matthew 6:25–30; Acts 17:28). God performs miracles (Exodus 4; John 2; 11; 20).	The scriptures of Judaism, Christianity, and Islam are theistic in viewpoint.	God possesses the omnipredicates (Psalm 139). God will conquer physical and spiritual evil (1 John 3:8; Colossians 2:14–15; Revelation 21:4).	God is infinite and transcendent (Psalm 139:7–12; Psalm 113:5–6; Jeremiah 23:23; Revelation 1:8). God is omnipotent (Genesis 18:14; Matthew 28:18). Though humans are dependent on God, God is not dependent on mankind (Genesis 1:27; 2:7; Exodus 3:14; Daniel 4:35; Acts 17:28; Isaiah 45:18).	God is personal and transcendent (Psalm 103:13; 113:5–6; Isaiah 55:8–9). God is distinct from creation (Romans 1:19–21).	There is only one true God (Deuteronomy 6:4). God has no competitors (Isaiah 43:10–11). The second commandment prohibits worship of anything in heaven or on earth (Exodus 20:4-5).
Proponents	Ayn Rand Friedrich Nietzsche Karl Marx Michael Martin Ludwig Feuerbach	Voltaire John Toland Thomas Paine Thomas Hobbes Charles Blount Antony Flew Lord Herbert of Cherbury	Augustine Avicenna M. Maimonides	Plato John Stuart Mill	Alfred North Whitehead Charles Hartshorne John Cobb Jr. Shubert Ogden Lewis Ford Henri Bergson Diogenes	D. T. Suzuki Radha Krishnan Benedictus de Spinoza Alan Watts G. W. F. Hegel	Joseph Smith Margo Adler

Chart 27

Classic Arguments for the Existence of God

Title	Argument	Proponent
Argument from Motion *a posteriori**	There is motion (locomotion) in the universe. Something cannot move itself; an external agent or force is required. An infinite regress of forces is meaningless. Hence, there must be a being who is the ultimate source of all motion while not being moved itself. This being is God, the unmoved mover.	Thomas Aquinas
Cosmological Argument (Argument from Cause) *a posteriori*	Every effect has a cause. There cannot be an infinite regress of finite causes. Therefore, there must be an uncaused cause or necessary being. This being is God.	Thomas Aquinas
Argument from Possibility and Necessity *a posteriori*	Things exist in a network of relationships to other things. They can exist only within this network. Therefore, each is a dependent thing. However, an infinite regress of dependencies is contradictory. There must, then, be a being who is absolutely independent, not contingent on anything else. This being is God.	Thomas Aquinas
Argument from Perfection *a posteriori*	It can be observed in the universe that there is a pyramid of beings (e.g., from insects to humans), in an ever-increasing degree of perfection. There must be a final being who is absolutely perfect, the source of all perfection. This being is God.	Thomas Aquinas
Teleological Argument (Argument from Design) *a posteriori*	There is an observable order or design in the world that cannot be attributed to the object itself (e.g., inanimate objects). This observable order argues for an intelligent being who established this order. This being is God.	Thomas Aquinas
Moral, or Anthropological, Argument *a posteriori*	All people possess a moral impulse or categorical imperative. Since this morality is not always rewarded in this life, there must be some basis or reason for moral behavior that is beyond this life. This implies the existence of immortality, ultimate judgment, and a God who establishes and supports morality by rewarding good and punishing evil.	Immanuel Kant
Argument That God Is an Innate Idea *a priori*†	All normal human beings are born with the idea of God implanted in the mind, though it is suppressed in unrighteousness (Romans 1:18). As the child grows into adulthood, this idea becomes clearer. Critical experiences in the course of life may make this idea come alive.	Augustine John Calvin Charles Hodge
Argument from Mysticism *a priori*	Mankind is able to have a direct mystical experience with God resulting in an ecstatic experience. This union with God is so uniquely overpowering that it self-validates the existence of God.	Evelyn Underhill

Chart 28

Classic Arguments for the Existence of God (continued)

Argument from Truth *a priori*	All people believe that something is true. If God is the God of truth and the true God, then God is Truth. This Truth (capital T) is the context for all other truth. Therefore, the existence of truth implies the existence of Truth, which implies the existence of God.	Augustine A. H. Strong
Ontological Argument *a priori*	*Major premise:* Mankind has an idea of an infinite and perfect being. *Minor premise:* Existence is a necessary part of perfection. *Conclusion:* An infinite and perfect being exists, since the very concept of perfection requires existence.	Anselm of Canterbury
Argument from Mankind's Finitude *a priori*	Humans are aware of their finitude. What makes them aware of this? God is continually impressing humans with God's infinitude. Therefore the sense of finitude itself is proof that an infinite being, God, exists.	Aristotle
Argument from Blessedness *a priori*	Humans are restless, with a vague longing for blessedness until they rest in God. This longing was given by God. The presence of this longing is an indirect proof of God's existence.	Augustine Thomas Aquinas
Argument from Perception *a priori*	Human beings are able to perceive (sense) things. This cannot be caused either by physical events (perception as a mental act) or by human beings themselves. Therefore, the existence of perception implies God's existence as the only rational explanation for human perceptions.	Bishop George Berkeley
Existential Argument *a priori*	God proves himself via the kerygma, which is his declaration of love, forgiveness, and justification of mankind. Those who decide for the kerygma then knows God exists. No other evidence is needed. God is not so much proven as he is known, and this occurs existentially, from experiences in life.	Auguste Sabatier

*a posteriori: statements or arguments that logically follow from, or are dependent on, sense experience.
†a priori: statements or arguments that are logically prior to, or independent of, sense experience.

Chart 28

Evaluation of Classic Arguments for the Existence of God

The Ontological Argument

This argument takes the following form:

Major premise: Mankind has an idea of an infinite and perfect being.

Minor premise: Existence is a necessary part of perfection.

Conclusion: An infinite and perfect being exists, since the very concept of perfection requires existence.

Proponent: Anselm of Canterbury

Against	For
Statements about existence cannot be necessary because necessity is merely a logical characteristic of propositions. There is no connection between the existence of a perfect being in a person's mind and the actual existence of that being in the world. The argument requires an adoption of a Platonic framework in which the ideal is more real than the physical.	If the statement "no statements about existence are necessary" is true, it must also apply to the statement itself, which would be self-defeating. Hence, it is possible that some necessary statements about existence can be made.

Cosmological Argument

Every effect has a cause; there cannot be an infinite regress of finite causes to account for currently existing effects (i.e., the universe); therefore, there must be an uncaused cause of all finite beings/things (effects); this cause of all being is God.

Proponents: Bonaventura, Thomas Aquinas, William Lane Craig

Against	For
There is no necessary connection (logically) between cause and effect. At best, we have only a psychological disposition to expect the effect to occur. A circle of causes may be an alternative to an infinite regress of causes.	The absence of an essential being or uncaused cause ultimately leads to self-creation or chance-creation, both of which are logically impossible. A circle or chain of causes would require a link in the chain to be causing existence and having its existence caused simultaneously, potentiality producing actuality, and this is not possible. Nothing cannot cause something (Genesis 1:1; Hebrews 3:4; Psalm 102:25–27).
The existence of an infinite Creator cannot be demonstrated from the existence of a finite universe.	A necessary being (i.e., a being that cannot not be) must be infinite. Only that which has potentiality can be limited, and a necessary being must be pure actuality (or else it could be possible for it not to exist).
If everything needs a cause, so does God, or else God must be self-caused, which is impossible.	The law of causality (every effect has a cause) applies only to finite beings. God, who is infinite and eternally self-existent, does not require a cause.

Chart 29

Evaluation of Classic Arguments for the Existence of God (continued)

The Teleological Argument

There is observable order or design in the world that cannot be accounted for by the object itself (e.g., inanimate objects); this observable order argues for an intelligent being who established this order; this being is God.

Proponents: William Paley, Thomas Aquinas

Against	For
The order in the world can be attributed to agents other than an intelligent being, such as chance or natural selection.	Creation by chance is equivalent to self-creation, for chance is a mathematical abstraction with no real existence in and of itself. Also, chance and eternity do not enhance the argument, since in a purely random arena things become more disorganized with time, not less (Psalm 19; Romans 1:19–21)
This argument fails to account for occurrences, such as natural catastrophes and disease, which argue against the existence of a good God.	Even in what appear to be random natural occurrences and in diseases, order is still present. The thrust of this argument is for the existence of an intelligent designer. It does not try to argue for the character of the designer.
This argument is invalid because it extends the observable to that which goes beyond experience.	This argument is *a posteriori*—from something outward, i.e., based upon observation. In view of the only alternative basis for postulating intelligent being, the *a priori*—from something inward—we have little choice but to base our arguments for God's existence on what we have observed in the world around us.

The Anthropological (Moral) Argument

All human beings possess a moral impulse or categorical (moral) imperative. Since this morality is not always rewarded in this life, there must be some basis or reason for moral behavior that is beyond this life. This implies the existence of immortality, ultimate judgment, and a God who establishes and supports morality by rewarding good and punishing evil.

Proponents: Immanuel Kant, C. S. Lewis

Against	For
The moral impulse of human beings may be attributed to sources other than God, such as the idea of conscience developing as a necessary part of the evolutionary process or of natural selection.	Since the conscience or moral impulse of human beings is often not in their best interests in terms of survival, it is unlikely that the conscience would develop as a necessary part of natural selection (Romans 2:14–16).
If God exists as a rewarder of good, why does evil exist (especially if, as theists profess, God is all good and all powerful)?	Though the existence of a God who is good (and all-powerful) may mandate the destruction of evil, it does not necessarily mandate that destruction now.
If this moral impulse comes from God's fiat alone, it is arbitrary and God is not essentially good (this militates against the good God of theism, for which this argument is used as proof).	This moral impulse is based on God's nature, not His arbitrary will. Indeed, God cannot be considered arbitrary because He cannot will contrary to His nature.

Chart 29

What Is God Like?

Classical Theism	
Metaphysical Attributes (non-communicable)	
Pure Dynamic Actuality	God is a pure being without any passive potential (i.e., ability to receive change to His nature). He cannot be anything more or less than He already is (Exodus 3:14; John 8:58).
Aseity	God is self-existent without any dependence on another for His very being. God is life and the ultimate source of all life (Exodus 3; 14; John 1:4).
Simplicity	God is one without any parts. He is uncompounded, incomplex, indivisible, unique, and essentially a Spirit being (John 1:18; 4:24; 1 Timothy 1:17; 6:15–16).
Unity	God is one (Deuteronomy 6:4; 1 Corinthians 8:6).
Infinity	God is without beginning, limits, termination, or finitude (1 Kings 8:27; Psalm 145:3; Acts 17:24).
Eternity	God endures eternally, wholly above and separate from the succession of time. God's eternity (ever-present now) encompasses all the characteristics of time (past, present, future) in one moment (Genesis 21:33; Psalm 90:2).
Immutability	Though God's activities (creation) change, He is unchangeable in His being (Numbers 23:19; Psalm 102:27; Malachi 3:6; James 1:17).
Omnipresence	God is everywhere present. He is active to and present at everything simultaneously, whether in time or in eternity (Psalm 139:7–12; Jeremiah 23:23–24).
Omniscience (Includes omnisapience, or wisdom)	God knows all actual and possible things immediately and from all eternity—including future human choices. The only things God cannot know are actual impossibilities, like "square circles" or "infinite finites." He simply knows these things as impossibilities according to His infinite and eternal mode of being (Psalms 139:1–4; 147:4–5; Matthew 11:27).
Omnipotence	God is all powerful but cannot do anything contrary to His nature, such as lie, deny Himself, change His mind, contradict Himself, or cease to exist (Malachi 3:6; 1 Samuel 15:29; Matthew 19:26; Hebrews 6:18; 7:21; Revelation 19:6).
Sovereignty	God is the supreme ruler, independent of any power or authority outside Himself.
Moral/Relational Attributes (communicable)	
Justice	God is equitable, whether it is demonstrated by punishment following from condemnation or grace leading to salvation. He does not show favoritism (Acts 10:34–35; Romans 2:11).
Love and Benevolence	God seeks the good of humans at His own infinite cost. God has unselfish concern and welfare for His creation (Deuteronomy 7:7–8; Psalm 103:17; John 3:16; Romans 5:6–8; Ephesians 2:4–5; 1 John 4:8, 10).

Chart 30

What Is God Like? (continued)

Grace	God extends undeserved favor to humans according to their need and His will (Exodus 34:6; Ephesians 1:5–8; Titus 2:11).
Goodness	Goodness constitutes the character of God. It is shown by His benevolence, mercy, and grace. His character is desirable for its own sake without being a means to an end. Rather it is the goal, ends, and purpose to which all ought to correspond and incline (Exodus 33:19; Psalm 145:9).
Freedom	God is a free agent, absolutely independent from all causal influence from His creatures (Psalm 115:3).
Holiness	God is righteous, perfect, set apart or separate from all sin or evil (Habakkuk 1:13; 1 Peter 1:16; 1 John 1:5).
Righteousness	Holiness is applied to relationships; God's law and actions are right (Psalm 19:7–9; Jeremiah 9:24).
Truth	Agreement and consistency with all that is represented by God Himself. That is, God's actions and thoughts perfectly correspond to His nature (Hebrews 6:19; Titus 1:2).
Genuineness	God is real and true without error or contradiction (John 1:14; 14:6; 17:3).
Veracity	God speaks the truth and is trustworthy (1 Samuel 15:29; John 17:17, 19; Hebrews 6:18; Titus 1:2).
Faithfulness	God proves true; He keeps His promises despite the unfaithfulness of His creatures (Numbers 23:19; Psalm 89:2; 1 Thessalonians 5:24).
Personality	God is personal. He possesses self-awareness, mind, will, and self-determination (Genesis 3; Exodus 3:14).
Impassibility	God cannot be changed or moved by anything outside Himself (Exodus 3:14).
Mercy	God is tenderhearted, showing compassion toward the miserable, demonstrating His love to mankind, and abstaining from bringing upon people what they deserve (Exodus 3:7, 17; Psalm 103:13; Matthew 9:36).
Persistence	God has a long-suffering nature and patience toward His people (Psalm 86:15; Romans 2:4; 9:22; 2 Peter 3:9).

Chart 30

Evil

	Question	Proposed Answer
Source	If God can create only good and perfect things, how then can evil come from what is totally perfect and good, whether it be from God or His created order?	Although it is true that God initially created everything good, one of the faculties God created in human beings was the ability to freely choose. Therefore, evil resulted as a by-product or concomitant of this freedom to choose. As such, God is an indirect cause of evil since He created humans with the potential for evil. The immediate cause of evil is mankind, who chose to sin.
Substance/Nature	If God directly created every spiritual and material substance, and evil is either spiritual or material, then God created evil. Therefore, God is to blame for all evil.	Although God created all spiritual and material substances, it has yet to be demonstrated that evil is a "substance" possessing materiality or form (nature) like those found in humans or angels. More precisely, according to Augustine, evil is a lack, absence, or corruption of what ought to be present in good substances.[1] Therefore, evil has no existence in itself, but exists similar to a parasite in a good host.
Longevity	The existence of an all-powerful and all-good God appears to be at odds with the persistence of evil. The fact that evil remains active in the world is an indicator that God cannot or will not destroy evil.	Since God possesses all power and goodness, He will defeat evil in the future. Simply because evil is not eradicated today does not necessarily mean it will not one day be overcome. God did defeat evil positionally through Christ and will defeat evil practically at His second coming.
God's Will	Since God determines all things, He must will all things, including evil. But if He wills evil, God must be evil. Alternatively, if God does not determine all things, including evil, He is not in control of the universe. Therefore, God must will evil.	According to Aquinas, God can will things in at least two ways. First, He can will that some things occur necessarily (no choice), such as His own existence. Second, other things He wills to occur conditionally (by free choice), such as our actions, whether evil or good. Thus it is humans who should be praised or blamed and held responsible for the effects that flow from their choices, since God does not will evil to occur or not to occur. Rather, God only wills to permit evil to occur.[2]
Avoidance	God appears to be sadistic since He knew omnisciently that evil would enter the world. God could have created a world in which it would be impossible for evil to flourish or abstained from creating a world altogether. Since he did not abstain implies either that God does not have all knowledge or that He lacks providential control of the world.	God created the best world in which to achieve His ultimate goals. This world includes creatures with freedom, which makes meaningful our love, actions, and salvation. However, with freedom there is an inherent potential for evil (just as there is the possibility of drowning when waterskiing). God could have created a world without freedom. However, the problem of meaningful choice and its relationship to responsibility emerges. To assert that somehow if God abstained from creating a world is better than a world where evil is present is reductionistic and seems to imply nothing is better than something. God has full providential control of the world because He knew evil would occur.

[1] Augustine, *On the Morals of the Manachaeans*, 5.7.

[2] Thomas Aquinas, *Summa Theologica*, I.19.8–9.

Chart 31

Views of Evil

Topic	Theism	Deism	Finitism	Atheism
Origin	By-product of freedom.	By-product of freedom (and ignorance).	Result of God's limited power.	Lack of knowledge/ education.
Nature	A lack or absence of what ought to be present, namely, wholeness.	Lack, or corruption, of the good.	Improper results and relations due to God's lack of providential control.	Sickness, disease, social and moral ills, lack of progress (ignorance).
Longevity	God has defeated evil judicially, or legally, and will defeat it practically.	Will continue until man or God eradicates evil.	No guarantee that evil will ever be defeated by God or man.	Evil will continue indefinitely or until man solves the problem.
Avoidability	Evil could have been avoided if finite beings made morally correct decisions.	Evil could have been avoided if finite beings made morally correct decisions according to the laws of nature and reason.	Avoidance of evil is improbable due to the finite nature of God and man, and no clear absolute moral standard.	If God knows all, including future evil, why did He create the world? Evil will only be avoided through the power of mankind.
Negative Consequences	Spiritual depravity which can eventuate in eternal death; physical privation.	Spiritual depravity which can eventuate in eternal death; physical privation.	Spiritual, social, material, or cosmological effects.	All consequences are temporally manifested as economic, organic, intellectual, biological, social, and scientific, but not spiritual.
Solution	Relationally, evil is overcome by faith in Christ alone. Practically, it will be defeated at Christ's second coming.	Evil is defeated by personal faith in Christ or by human reason that affords solutions to social and moral ills.	No guaranteed solution. God and man will attempt to overcome evil as they both struggle to bring the world into subjection.	Education, science, and development of human potential will alleviate the effects of evil.
Final State	Evil will be quarantined in hell and forever separated from good (in heaven).	Evil will be eternally separated from good.	No guarantee of final state or condition of evil since God does not possess all power to assure victory.	Eventually evil will be eradicated by man's efforts in education, science, and legislation.

Chart 32

Views of Evil (continued)

Topic	Polytheism	Pantheism	Panentheism	
Origin	By-product of warfare between the gods and lack of appeasement.	Originated as an illusion; attachment to worldly desires causes suffering.	Results from God's imperfect relation with the world.	
Nature	Evil is described as not gaining the intended results; lack of proper relationships among the gods and between the gods and people.	Described as ignorance; lack of self-knowledge; suffering.	Evil is not fitting into God's creativity; incompatibility.	
Longevity	Evil will remain indefinitely since no one god or man possesses absolute power to totally eradicate evil.	Since evil has no real extra-mental existence, it will endure as long as one's perception of being remains convinced of the distinction of evil.	Since God's creativity has infinite potential, evil will also endure infinitely.	
Avoidability	Avoidance of evil cannot be guaranteed due to the finite and limited nature of the gods. Mankind's best way to avoid evil is by appeasement.	Evil could have been avoided if man did not have the capacity for ignorance of self-identity.	Avoidance of evil cannot be guaranteed due to the finite and limited nature of God's body (actual pole).	
Negative Consequences	Natural and spiritual chaos.	Lack of a proper view of reality, resulting in imbalance and disharmony, which can create relational and societal problems.	Evil is not compatible with God's process, thus negatively impacting God's spiritual and social life.	
Solution	Appease the gods.	Self-realization that God and man are one without distinction.	No solution to evil; God and the world attempt to actualize every potential without being incompatible with God's creativity and goals.	
Final State	Evil cannot be defeated due to the limited power of both the gods and mankind.	God and evil will eventually be overcome due to universal self-consciousness which leads to merger/absorption of evil back into God.	Evil cannot be finally overcome due to God's and mankind's essentially finite condition.	

Chart 32

Theories of God's Relationship to Evil

Topic	Explanation	Proponents
Illusionism	There is no extra-mental reality of evil. Evil is defined in terms of imbalance, error of the mind, or altogether illusory.	Parmenides Zeno Mary Baker Eddy Some forms of Buddhism, Hinduism
Dualism	Acknowledges the reality of evil in the world. In Zoroastrianism it is understood in terms of an eternal never-ending cosmic struggle between the good (Ahura Mazda) and the evil (Angra-Mainyu).	Zoroastrianism Manichaenism
Determinism	Maintains that evil is real and that God had no other option available to His creative potential. Since God is a necessary being, His creation (our world) necessarily issues from Him the same way ripples in a pond necessarily flow outward from a central point of contact.	Plotinus Benedictus de Spinoza
Impossibilism	Evil is real. God created the world freely along with creatures who possess freedom (self-determination). However, God did not/cannot know future contingent events; therefore, it is impossible for God to know how free creatures would use their freedom. Since God controls all things that are not free, it would be impossible to control evil, which springs from human freedom.	Openness theology
Finitism	Asserts that evil is real. Because God is limited in power and/or goodness he therefore cannot overcome it.	William James John Stuart Mill Charles Hartshorne
Malevolence	Although this view is rare, evil is viewed as real. God in some way enjoys the privation, pain, and suffering of His creatures.	Perhaps held by emotionally scarred and/or disgruntled individuals
Realism	Asserts that evil is a real lack, corruption, or privation in good substances. Though Christ has defeated evil judicially, God, as an omnipotent and omnibenevolent being, can and will in the future defeat evil practically.	Augustine Thomas Aquinas Classical theism

Chart 33

PART 4
RELIGIOUS
APOLOGETICS

Theories on the Origin of Religion

Religious View	Explanation	Evaluation	Proponents
Subjective/ Projection/ Psychological Theory	Approaches the origin of religion from a psychological phenomenon rather than an objective Being within a historical construct. Religion resides in the seat of a person's emotions and feelings and is an outgrowth of one's psychological need. Explains religion in terms of symbols and behavior instead of dogmatic descriptions. An extra-mental "God" is not assumed as an object of faith since religion begins at the subconscious level, thus is viewed entirely as an intrinsic self-contained phenomenon. Proponents of the subjective theory often differ in their psychological emphasis. For example, Schleiermacher begins with absolute dependence, Feuerbach suggests that man worships an idealized self-image, Freud claimed religion was an idealized father image, Otto asserted religion was an encounter with the feeling of holiness, and Jung defined it in terms of images or archetypes that recur in dreams.	Proponents of this theory cannot be faulted for attempting to explain the origins of religion. The theory has been commended for acknowledging that religion is not entirely a doctrinal exercise. Instead, relationships and the subjective element ought not to be neglected. Nevertheless, there are several issues which are problematic. The theory ignores the historical evidence compiled by religionists. The tendency to eliminate the existence of God because of an inner origin of religion neglects the possibility that maybe God placed the religious need within humans. The reliance on "inner" criteria as a test for truth is problematic since it lacks any objective data by which to discover the truth of the theory. How do we know that these "feelings" or "needs" are really related to how one views God? One could simply assert that the subjectivist must have a psychological need to lie about the origin of religion.	Friedrich Schleiermacher Ludwig Feuerbach Sigmund Freud Rudolph Otto Carl Jung
Evolutionary Theory	Popularized during the rise of Darwin's theory of evolution. Religion is viewed as progressing through various evolutionary stages of development, beginning with the most primitive expression, called "mana," which is the awareness of an invisible supernatural power or force in nature. Subsequent development into ancestor worship, polytheism (many gods), and monotheism (one God) is thought to be the result of increased religious sophistication among developing peoples. This theory is largely driven by a commitment to Darwin's theory of evolution and cultural anthropology.	The evolutionary theory has been credited for attempting to investigate the historical origins and changes within religious expression. However, serious problems still remain. According to religionist Winfried Corduan, religion has never been observed to follow a strict evolutionary pattern. Change within religion is not uniform; rather it has been observed moving in all directions. Many theorists assume an evolutionary view of life and have illegitimately transferred this questionable concept to the study of religion. After all, some current primitive cultures may have devolved from earlier sophistication. Several modern studies, such as Wilhelm Schmidt's *The Origin and Growth of Religion: Facts and Theories*, have theorized that early cultures believed in one high god above all others, which is a direct challenge to religious evolutionary theory.	Charles Darwin Edward Burnett Tylor James Frazer

Chart 34

Theories on the Origin of Religion (continued)

Original Monotheism Theory	Asserts that God is the primary source of religion. Wilhelm Schmidt is well known for collecting data from the major continents of the world. The information he gathered indicated an early belief in a high sky God. In the most ancient cultures of Africa and Australia, Schmidt discovered that there was a strong worship of God without the practice of magic, which is the opposite conclusion of the evolutionary approach. The Abrahamic religions of Judaism, Christianity, and Islam would assert that at the beginning of creation there was only God, and subsequently mankind disobeyed His guidance and will. In the classical theism of Augustine, Anselm, and Aquinas, and in Islam and Judaism, this God is one, eternal, self-existing, merciful, and compassionate. In contrast to the evolutionary approach, original monotheism suggests that instead of evolving to a belief in one God, there has been a devolution on a personal and/or cultural level from God. This departure is random in the direction of henotheism, polytheism, and animism.	Proponents of original monotheism should be acknowledged for investigating and appreciating the historical and relational aspects of religion. Their comprehensive treatment of the subject has offered ample information to supplement additional research in the field of religious studies. Some have criticized some proponents of original monotheism for their findings of bias in research even though it seems that all researchers have bias. The real question would more importantly address whether one's bias is good or bad, or true or false. Others suggest that original monotheism is contrary to established data concerning the theory of evolution and modern cultural anthropology.	Augustine Thomas Aquinas Anselm of Canterbury Wilhelm Schmidt Christianity Islam Judaism

This chart contains some information found in Winfried Corduan, *Neighboring Faiths* (Downers Grove, Ill.: InterVarsity Press, 1998).

Chart 34

Comparison of Creation Accounts

	The Bible	Egypt	Sumer	Akkad[1]	Iran	China	Japan
Creator	Elohim Yahweh	Atum, Shu, Tefnut, Gen, Nut, Osiris	Enlil, Ninlil, Nusku, Nunbarshegunu	Tiamat, Apsu, Ea, Marduk	Ahriman, Ohrmazd, the Amahraspands	Heaven, Earth, P'an-ku	Eight pairs of deities, Izanagi, Izanami
Means	Man fashioned from dust, woman made from man	Copulation, hierarchy of gods	Rape, self-glorification	Murder of other gods by Marduk	War between the gods, creation from a humanoid body	Death of a god	Copulation, incest, violence
View of Mankind	Crown of creation, intended to rule over it and take dominion.	Descended from gods, meant to serve them.	Gods fashion from mud six types of abnormal humans who are made to do the work of the gods.	Made from the blood of slain god(s) mixed with the clay of Mesopotamia; created to till land and build temples for all time.	Ohrmazd creates Gayomart (the first man), who is defiled by his union with the first woman. Masya and Masyanag come from seed of Gayomart.	Parasites on the body of a god are impregnated by the wind and become human beings.	Humans live out the lessons of the gods.
Sources	Genesis 1-3	Pyramid Texts	"Enlil and the Creation of the Pickaxe," "Summer and Winter"	"Enuma Elish"	Pahlavi Texts: The Bundahisn	San-wu li-chi (The P'an-ku myth)	Ko-ji-ki Nihon-gi
Comparison to Biblical Account	The prototype: Monotheistic, man is peak of creation, fall with promise of hope, consistent morality, God is infinite, just, personal, transcendent, and perfect.	Polytheistic, human hierarchy, mortal and amoral gods	Polytheistic, debased activity among the gods, humans as slaves, low view of mankind, immoral	Polytheistic, nature-based, humans enslaved to the gods, violent, low view of mankind	Polytheistic, low view of women, immoral, superstitious, nature-based, animistic	Polytheistic, low view of mankind, amoral, nature-based, develops toward animistic	Polytheistic, immoral, negligent of mankind, violent, animistic

Adapted from Ken M. Durham, 1988. Dallas Seminary Lay Institute Survey of Bible Backgrounds. Used by permission.
David and Margaret Adams-Leeming, *A Dictionary of Creation Myths* (New York: Oxford University Press, 1996).
C. Scott Littleton, ed., *Mythology: The Illustrated Anthology of World Myth and Storytelling* (Holt, Mich.: Thunder Bay, 2002).
Barbara C. Sproul, *Primal Myths: Creation Myths Around the World* (reprint, San Francisco: Harper San Francisco, 1979).
Roy Willis, ed., *World Mythology* (reprint, New York: Owl, 1996).

[1] Akkad was a city in ancient Mesopotamia, which was at its peak in the 24th to 22nd centuries BC. In Genesis 10:10 Akkad is mentioned in a list of cities. Some have speculated that it was located on the Euphrates River in what is now Iraq, southwest of Baghdad.

Chart 35

Evolutionary View of the Origin of Religion

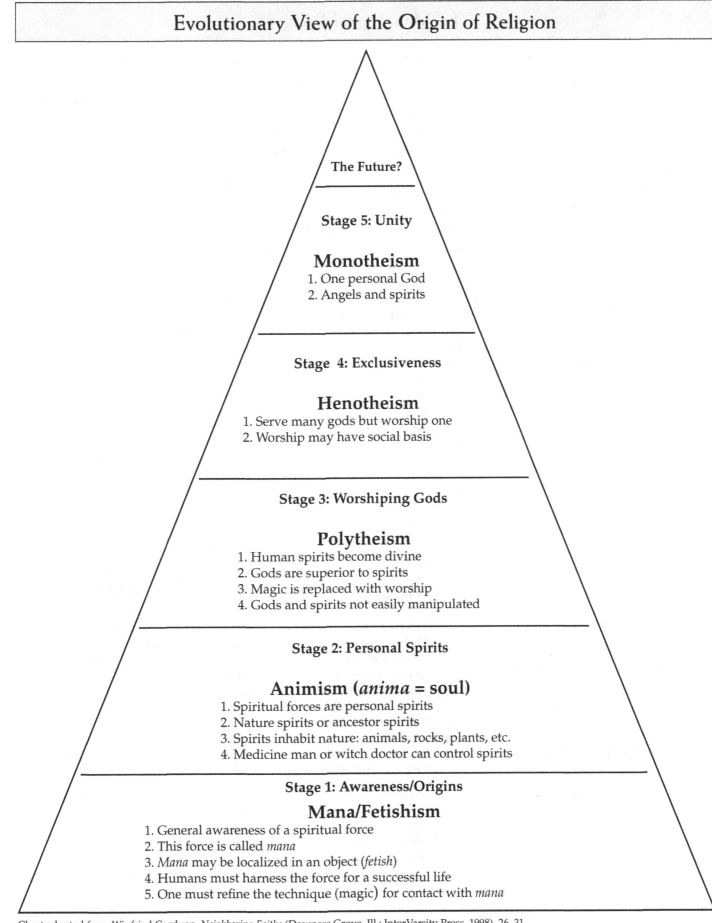

The Future?

Stage 5: Unity

Monotheism
1. One personal God
2. Angels and spirits

Stage 4: Exclusiveness

Henotheism
1. Serve many gods but worship one
2. Worship may have social basis

Stage 3: Worshiping Gods

Polytheism
1. Human spirits become divine
2. Gods are superior to spirits
3. Magic is replaced with worship
4. Gods and spirits not easily manipulated

Stage 2: Personal Spirits

Animism (*anima* = soul)
1. Spiritual forces are personal spirits
2. Nature spirits or ancestor spirits
3. Spirits inhabit nature: animals, rocks, plants, etc.
4. Medicine man or witch doctor can control spirits

Stage 1: Awareness/Origins

Mana/Fetishism
1. General awareness of a spiritual force
2. This force is called *mana*
3. *Mana* may be localized in an object (*fetish*)
4. Humans must harness the force for a successful life
5. One must refine the technique (magic) for contact with *mana*

Chart adapted from Winfried Corduan, *Neighboring Faiths* (Downers Grove, Ill.: InterVarsity Press, 1998), 26–31.

Chart 36

The Meaning of Religion

These individuals are important figures since the Enlightenment who greatly influenced development of the current liberal meaning of the nature of religion in the West.

Individual	Date	View of Religion	Literary Work
Friedrich Schleiermacher	1768–1834	According to Schleiermacher, religion is not a set of beliefs and doctrines or confined to morality; instead it is the primordial feeling of absolute dependence, which everyone possesses and which he describes as inescapable. If there is a feeling of dependence, there must be an object toward which it depends, namely, God. For Schleiermacher, the subjective feeling precedes its object, God.	*On Religion: Speeches to Its Cultured Despisers* *The Christian Faith*
Ludwig Feuerbach	1804–1872	Feuerbach's influential works describe God as an idealized figure who can help fulfill human needs, desires, and wishes. God is created in the image of man in an effort to provide ourselves with one on whom humanity may depend. As people become empowered, religion becomes obsolete or at least less necessary.	*The Essence of Christianity* *The Essence of Religion*
Karl Marx	1818–1883	Marx, an avowed atheist, follows Feuerbach by asserting that "man makes religion, religion does not make man." Man simply projects his ideas and imagination to form an "ultimate reality" to which he can relate. Marx departs from Feuerbach in that he sees the origin and nature of religion in terms of economic and social struggles. Whereas those who came before Marx interpreted and defined religion, Marx seems to have been preoccupied with the desire to eradicate religion through realizing an environment characteristic of a socialistic utopia.	*Marx and Engels on Religion*
Herbert Spencer	1820–1903	Spencer theorized that the dreams of primitive peoples about their recently deceased relatives and/or friends provide the basis for the development of their concept of gods. This theory he called mana, meaning "spirit" or "ghost."	*Principles of Sociology*
Max Muller	1823–1900	Muller, an Oxford professor, posited that religion developed as a result of primitive man's observation of natural forces. These forces were subsequently personalized and worshiped and became the object of created mythology.	*Science of Language*
R. H. Codrington	1830–1922	During his time as a Christian missionary in Melanesia, Codrington theorized that all primitive people began with mana, a simple awareness of a power or force in nature. This power was initially experienced through the subjective emotions rather than objectively through the intellect.	*The Melanesians*
Edward Burnett Tylor	1832–1917	Tylor believed that primitive cultures developed a sense of "otherness" and "soul" as a result of one's experiences with death and dreams. Eventually these souls were believed to be located in natural objects such as rocks and rivers. With the power to help or harm, these souls became the object of appeasement and flattery.	*Primitive Cultures*

Chart 37

The Meaning of Religion (continued)

James George Frazer	1854–1941	Through his study of the works of various anthropologists and historians, Frazer concluded that there was an evolutionary development of religion in three stages. Man attempted to manipulate nature through various techniques, which resulted in discouragement when nature would not cooperate. Man used religion in an effort to request the cooperation of nature. Modern man does not rely on religion, but on science, to meet his needs.	*The Golden Bough*
Sigmund Freud	1856–1939	By exploring the subconscious level, Freud viewed religion as the fulfillment of a desire for a father image. This desire or need appears to be the result of guilt experienced for hating one's father. Ultimately religion is a sign of neurosis and psychological immaturity. People who are strong and healthy can preserve their own well-being.	*Totem and Taboo* *Future of an Illusion*
Emile Durkheim	1858–1917	Durkheim, a French sociologist, was the first to suggest that religion is not necessarily worship, belief, and miracles ascribed to a particular deity but objects in a community that are deemed sacred. Since it is society that ascribes value to the objects, each community may differ in what is acknowledged as absolute.	*The Elementary Forms of the Religious Life*
Wilhelm Schmidt	1868–1954	Schmidt's comprehensive research analyzed primitive cultures around the world, which led him to disagree with Tylor, Muller, and others. He discovered that there was a consistent belief in a high God that possessed the omnipredicates (omniscience, omnisapience, omnipresence, omnipotence, etc.), morality, and benevolence. Even among primitive animistic and polytheistic cultures he found an original belief in one powerful God above his rivals.	*The Origin and Growth of Religion: Facts and Theories*
Rudolf Otto	1869–1937	Otto emphasizes the belief that religion is understood in terms of psychological experience, in particular, the feeling of holiness. An encounter with holy reality comes as one experiences awe, dread, and attraction while being smothered with the consciousness of God's greatness. As a result, one realizes his/her own lack of greatness and significance in comparison to the consciousness of holiness.	*The Idea of the Holy*
Carl G. Jung	1875–1961	Though Jung differed in some respects from his colleague Sigmund Freud, he maintained that religion resides in the seat of the human unconscious. Images called "archetypes" reside in the collective unconscious, appear to recur in dreams, and manifest themselves in religion, myth, and fairytales. Religion is viewed as an instrument through which much can be learned about human nature and the environment of humans.	*Psychology of the Unconscious*

Chart 37

World Religions

Topic	Judaism	Christianity	Islam
Reality	God created the universe out of nothing (*ex nihilo*) and every existing thing depends on Him for its preservation in being. Heaven and hell are literal places to which one goes after death.	God created the universe *ex nihilo*. He is the preserving cause of all reality by His power. Heaven and hell are literal abodes after death.	God (Allah) is the creator, designer, and sustainer of the universe. Heaven for faithful Muslims and hell for all others.
Objections	Pantheists, who believe that God and the universe are one and the same, challenge the distinction between creator and creation. They reason that since God is viewed as a "necessary" being, He must necessarily have emanated Himself. The Jewish concept of creation from nothing and the universe's subsequent dependence on its creator is contradictory to the pantheist view because it implies a choice in the creative event. This is not acceptable to the pantheist since it implies a *choice* to create instead of creation by necessity occurring apart from any decision by a personal divine being.	Secular views suggest chance and time (big bang and naturalistic evolution) as an explanation of design in the universe. The secular view also disagrees on individual responsibility, putting the focus in terms of society, environment, culture, and personality instead of on personal decisions and giving account of one's life to God. Secular humanists also reject Christianity's promise of an afterlife.	As a theistic religion, Islam has been subjected to the same criticisms as Judaism and Christianity. See objections under Judaism and Christianity.
Revelation	The Hebrew scriptures (Tanakh), composed of the Torah (Law), Prophets, and Writings.	The Bible, both Old and New Testaments, consisting of 66 books written by 40 different authors in three languages on three continents over a period of 1,500 years.	Primarily the Qur'an. However, other holy books consist of the Torah (*Tawrat*), Psalms (*Zabur*) and the Gospels (*Injil*).
Objections	Some suggest that the Hebrew scriptures smack of favoritism and racism, since the "Jews" are chosen to be God's people to the exclusion of other ethnic groups. Others question the historical reliability, authenticity, and Mosaic authorship of the written records.	One argument is that the Bible reflects ancient culture and cannot be adopted as literal for modern man. A higher critical approach to biblical studies has marshaled arguments against the historical and textual integrity of the manuscript copies, since the originals (autographs) are not available for scrutiny.	Despite Muslim claims that the Qur'an is perfect, several Muslim and non-Muslim scholars have charged it with grammatical irregularities and historical inaccuracies. Muslim scholar Ali Dashti states in his book *Twenty-Three Years* that there are "sentences which are incomplete and not fully intelligible without the aid of commentaries;... adjectives and verbs inflected without observance of the concords of gender and number; illogically and ungrammatically applied pronouns which sometimes have no referent." Gleason Archer identified several historical inaccuracies, one of which is described in Surah 20:87–94, which blames the golden calf incident in Exodus 32 (13th to 15th century BC) on a particular "samiri/samari" (Samaritan). Samaritans did not exist until the 6th century BC.

Chart 38

World Religions (continued)

Topic	Judaism	Christianity	Islam
God	Monotheistic: God is one. The divine attributes include the omnipredicates: perfect benevolence, eternality, infinity, immanence, self-existence, and sovereignty.	Monotheistic: God is one in nature, yet three distinct divine persons exist: Father, Son, and Holy Spirit. He possesses the omnipredicates: is supremely good, eternal, infinite, immanent, self-existent, and exercises His providence over the entire world.	Monotheistic: There is only one God, "Allah." Allah possesses the omnipredicates and aseity, is merciful, eternal, and transcendent, and hates evil.
Objections	Atheism and some forms of Buddhism suggest there is no credible evidence to support the existence of a personal God, nor can theism adequately explain the problem of evil and suffering in the world in light of the existence of a benevolent, all-powerful being. Christians have pointed out that the Hebrew word used for "one" (*echad*) in Deuteronomy 6:4 to describe the oneness of God allows for plurality in the Godhead. The author did not use the other Hebrew word *yacheed* to denote the absolute oneness of God (cf. *elohim*).	Non-Christian religions criticize the Trinity for being contradictory since it is impossible to have three persons in one God at the same time and in the same sense. The word "Trinity" is not found in the Bible; it is a term developed several hundred years later. According to some, the Christian concept of a triune God was most likely not due to new revelation but rather a result of pagan influence by earlier cultures espousing triadic theology. Many of the traditional arguments pertaining to God's existence have been deemed invalid, antiquated, and/or fail to overcome insurmountable philosophical and scientific difficulties.	Though God is explained in terms of personality, it appears that Allah possesses a nature that is unknowable to his followers since nothing in the finite world resembles him by way of analogy. Some insist this leads to agnosticism along with the view that Allah is in some sense detached and distant from his creation. Though unknowable in essence, Allah does reveal his will, thus placing stress on obedience rather than relationship. The emphasis on Allah's will has led to the charge that followers are merely slaves to a taskmaster.
Mankind	Mankind was created in God's image with certain communicable characteristics, rebelled against God and became sinful and needs God's forgiveness to be restored to a state of fellowship with Him.	Mankind was created in the image and likeness of God and has communicable attributes. Mankind's rebellion against God caused human nature to be fallen. Everyone, therefore, is a sinner and needs redemption.	Mankind is basically good, not sinful by nature, and can and should live in submission to Allah.
Objections	Islam argues that there is nothing that resembles God (Allah) in any way due to the infinite nature of His being and the finite nature of creation. Secular humanism insists it is impossible for miracles (creation) to occur and, to explain human development as evolutionary processes, presents evidence from science—transitional fossils, carbon dating, and similarities in animal and human genetics.	The Christian doctrine of mankind as "sinner" who has violated God's moral law has been rejected on several fronts. Determinists assert that man's actions are caused by an internal or external force, whether environmental or spiritual, although some claim actions can arise spontaneously without a cause. Both would free individuals of any responsibility for their actions. Since there exists the inherent power to choose, one whose actions are self-caused can be considered responsible.	Though Muslims view mankind as inherently good, as stated in the Qu'ran, they have difficulty explaining why everyone falls short of perfection. An inconsistency exists with other accepted holy books, such as the Tawrat, Zabur, and Injil, which contain passages that describe the inherent sinfulness of mankind. Critics also have identified a problem in reconciling the strong determinism spoken of in the Qur'an (17:13) and mankind's responsibility for their choices (18:29).
Sin/Evil	Sin originated in the heart of a fallen angel known as the Devil or Satan. Sin is real and has both personal and social aspects.	Sin originated in the heart of Satan and is real. All human beings are sinners by nature and are in need of salvation. People are morally responsible for their sinful actions.	Sin consists of rejecting right guidance, yet mankind is deemed basically good. Forgiveness of sin is granted via repentance, but no atonement is necessary for salvation.

Chart 38

World Religions (continued)

Topic	Judaism	Christianity	Islam
Objections	The theory that sin/evil originated in the heart of an originally all-good being (Lucifer) is philosophically impossible, since evil cannot come from what is wholly good any more than one can extract apple juice from an orange. The cause cannot give what it does not possess.	Opponents point out that an all-loving God would not have created a world in which evil was possible unless he was powerful enough to conquer it. Yet evil is real and persistent with no signs of diminution. Therefore, God either lacks love and/or the power to overcome evil, making God limited and finite. The same arguments against Judaism's view of evil also apply to Christianity.	Most critics see a severe problem relating to the relationship between Allah's will and mankind's actions since Islam appears to have adopted the philosophy that "something is good if Allah wills it" instead of "something being good, therefore Allah wills it." If Allah's will to determine what is good is supreme to the exclusion of any grounding essence, then traditionally evil actions can be deemed good depending on Allah's will.
Salvation	Salvation can be obtained by doing good works, but sacrifices also are needed. One's good works are weighed against one's evil deeds.	Salvation can be obtained only by placing one's faith in the person and finished work of Jesus Christ, who died to atone for everyone's sins.	Salvation is based on human effort and can be obtained by one's good deeds.
Objections	Judaism appears to offer unclear criteria for salvation. For example, if animal sacrifice was needed to obtain salvation in the past, why are not sacrifices offered today? If works are necessary for salvation, how does one know when enough work has been completed? How can a finite amount of works be sufficient payment for an infinite debt (i.e., sin against an infinite God)? Why is the current religious system different from the one described in the Hebrew Scriptures?	Although most religions give positive marks to Jesus as a moral teacher, many object to the exclusive nature of salvation offered by Christianity. This exclusivism is viewed as elevating Christ to a superior position in relation to other faiths. The absence of works in salvation is criticized as offering an "easy believism" with no practical benefits to the here and now.	Salvation by obedience and good works appears to be unclear and incomplete since the quantity and quality of obedience/works can change due to the nature of Allah's will, which may change from time to time. Allah does not appear to have an essence or nature that grounds his will. This has led to the claim that Allah in his salvific requirements is arbitrary and/or capricious.
Time	God created time when he created the physical universe. The totality of time—past, present, and future—is finite.	God created time along with space and matter. Time is finite and has past, present, and future aspects.	Allah created time that is finite in nature.
Objections	Most agree that time is finite, but some argue that the future is not part of time since it has no actual existence. Others suggest that time is eternal in that it has no beginning or end but does possess successive change from one moment to another.	Eastern religions have questioned Christianity's linear view of time in favor of their cyclical view fueled by karma and reincarnation. It is said that clear concepts in the Bible, such as "born again," "rebirth," and "sowing and reaping" suggest a cyclical view of time that has been ignored or dismissed by Christians.	The Islamic view of time is subjected to the same criticism as Judaism and Christianity.
Other Religions	Judaism is exclusivistic in outlook, claiming to be the only true religion.	Though other religions may contain aspects of truth, only God's revelation as expressed in Jesus Christ and the Bible provide sufficient truth for salvation and a proper understanding of God.	Islam is exclusivistic, asserting that it alone is the true religion.

Chart 38

World Religions (continued)

| Objections | Judaism is criticized for being intolerant toward those with other religious viewpoints. | Christians are characterized as intolerant and narrow-minded because of their absolute view of truth and morality. Critics believe truth and morality are developed by culture and personal insight rather than given or mandated by God. | Some suggest that Islamic exclusivism has led to an intolerance that breeds violence in clashes with other faiths. Several passages in the Qu'ran have been interpreted as calls to violent behavior on ethnic and theological grounds (Surah 4:101; 5:51; 9:5, 29; 47:4). Despite these passages, the majority of the 1 billion Muslims worldwide live in peace. |

Topic	Secular Humanism	Hinduism	Buddhism
Reality	Universe consists solely of matter, energy, space, and time. It resulted from the big bang, the cause either unknown or unnecessary.	The universe is an unconscious emanation of divinity and has no beginning. Brahman is the only true ultimate reality.	The Buddha himself never described the world. However, Mahayana Buddhists hold that the universe consists of a series of heavens leading to nirvana.
Objections	Secular cosmogony has been challenged on many fronts. First, a purely material universe appears to be at odds with well-known immaterial realities. For example, numbers, knowledge, values, virtue, mind, logic, and time are all real yet are not composed of matter. Second, the secular view of origins lacks an adequate first cause to account for the development of life, order, intelligence, and morality.	Though Hindus claim the universe is unconscious and eternal, one's experience says otherwise. If the universe is unconscious, why are there conscious animals and humans? To answer the question by assuming one's senses are deceived is self-defeating since one must use senses to deny the senses' information. Hindus escape a threat in oncoming traffic by perceiving that threat with one or more of the senses. To claim that the universe is an illusion is equally unsatisfactory because one would need to know what reality is (something Hindus say is indescribable) in order to identify what, by contrast, is an illusion. The second law of thermodynamics shows that the entire universe is running out of usable energy and tending toward disorder (entropy). If this is the case and there is no distinction between Brahman and the universe, then Brahman is running out of energy. Whatever is running down cannot be infinite since an infinite being cannot run out of energy.	Theistic religions have questioned the soundness of Buddhism's approach to reality, that behind the phenomenal world nothing exists (*sunyata*), not even the *self* (*anatman*). Although it may be possible to dismiss the phenomenal world as an illusion, it is more difficult to deny one's own existence since the individual must exist in order to deny their own existence. Further, the denial of the phenomenal world is difficult as well because of the prior knowledge one must possess before making an absolute negation. One cannot say the world is "not real" (illusion) unless the individual possesses some knowledge of what, by contrast, "is real."
Revelation	No supernatural divine revelation exists. Truth is obtained through scientific observation and human reasoning. Major ideological expressions are found in the *Humanist Manifestos* I, II, and III.	The most important holy script (in most schools) is the *Bhagavad Gita*.	The first Buddhist scripture was the *Palicanon*. Although named after the language in which it is written, it is commonly called the *Tripitaka* (or *Tipitaka*).

Chart 38

World Religions (continued)

Topic	Secular Humanism	Hinduism	Buddhism
Objections	The *Humanist Manifestos* I and II have been criticized for their overly optimistic view of man's inherent goodness and the elevation of the scientific method as the supreme test of what is true. Recent wars and atrocities demonstrate the depravity of which man is capable. Humanism does not adequately acknowledge the immaterial and moral foundation on which science rests (honesty, virtue, knowledge), which itself cannot be tested by the scientific method of repeated observation. Some have suggested that science itself cannot be tested by the scientific method, implying that its basis is philosophical and moral, not empirical and repeatable.	The Bhagavad Gita, as well as the bulk of Hindu scripture, usually lacks any significant historical confirmation of persons, places, and events described. Although Hindus respond that history is largely unimportant, this is unsatisfactory since Krishna, as well as other incarnations of Vishnu, are either real or they are not. There is no archaeological or bibliographical evidence to support the claim that they are real. Why should anyone believe that Vishnu is real or, for that matter, believe in the reality of Brahman. What evidence exists to prove the teachings of Hinduism accurately correspond to reality?	Some contend that since the scriptures (*Tripitaka*) were originally conveyed orally and passed on for 100 to 300 years without being written, the confidence in what Siddhārtha Gautama (the Buddha) said is debatable. Recent changes and additions to Buddhist scripture suggest the possibility of early change and/or corruption. Some challenge the content of the scripture itself as being in some ways incoherent, illogical, unverifiable, and pessimistic.
God	God does not exist. The concept of God is merely a human-cultural invention. Philosophies like naturalism and materialism accurately describe reality.	Brahman is the monistic all-encompassing impersonal principle or force that resides in all things (pantheism). There exist many personal manifestations or incarnations (polytheism) of this impersonal force to which Hindus are encouraged to offer devotion or worship. The three more well-known chief gods are Brahma, Shiva, and Vishnu. In some cases God/gods are seen as amoral.	Atheistic in terms of practice. Buddha never denied the existence of a Supreme Being, but he thought that belief in God was not edifying for the religious life.

Chart 38

World Religions (continued)

Topic	Secular Humanism	Hinduism	Buddhism
Objections	Philosophers and theologians have offered several arguments for the existence of God. The cosmological argument states that "every effect must have a cause; since the universe is an effect, it must have a cause." The design argument asserts that "design implies a designer, the universe manifests design, therefore the universe has a designer." The moral argument states that moral law implies a moral-law giver, there is moral law, therefore, a moral-law giver exists.	Several arguments have been marshaled against the Hindu doctrine of God. The identification of Brahman as inexpressible, unknowable, and beyond knowledge appears to be self-defeating since each of these terms is descriptive of Brahman. Though Brahman is eternal, unchangeable, and identical to the universe, it is necessary for humans to free themselves from the cycle of reincarnation by a change of consciousness. However, this change would be impossible if Brahman is identical to the world and changeless. Thus, either God changes and is therefore finite, or man changes and is distinct from an unchanging Brahman. The adoption of either alternative would be a major departure from the traditional Hindu doctrine of ultimate reality.	Buddhism has avoided any speculation about the existence of metaphysical reality (God). However, if the Buddhist acknowledges it is impossible to deny one's own self-existence, the remaining question to ask would be "What kind of being/existence am I?" If the answer is an *infinite* kind of being, then the individual *is* God, thus refuting the claim that God does not exist. If the answer is a *finite* kind of being, then it (being) needs a cause, and this cause theism calls God. In addition, the traditional arguments for the existence of God would demonstrate that this God is infinitely powerful, intelligent, and moral. It may well be objected that it is possible for more than one God, instead there can be two or more infinite Gods. However, this appears to be unsatisfying since "two" Gods implies that there are differences between them; if there were no differences, they would be identical (one). The Greek philosopher Parmenides said, "to differ by nothing is not to differ at all." If there are differences between them, one God would *lack* what the other possessed. However, "lack" implies limitation and finitude, something an ultimate first cause (God) cannot have.
Mankind	Humans are a complex conglomeration of molecules, the end result of an evolutionary process that has progressed from single-celled organisms to higher forms of life.	The self is an illusion. Mankind undergoes many cycles of reincarnation. Human souls have always existed and are eternal.	Mankind goes through many cycles of reincarnation, yet it is maintained by many schools that the self is an illusion.

Chart 38

World Religions (continued)

Topic	Secular Humanism	Hinduism	Buddhism
Objections	In evaluating evolution, several problems emerge. Answers to philosophical questions regarding origins are often unclear or remain unanswered. For instance, How can life come from a non-living cause? How can intelligence come from non-intelligent causes? How does order emerge from non-order? How can something come from nothing? Evolution seems to lack transitional forms linking mankind to animals. Michael Behe in his *Darwin's Black Box*, offers a strong argument called "irreducible complexity," which denies the probability of cellular evolution occurring in incremental stages.	This doctrine has come under considerable attack from Western culture in general and theistic religions in particular. Describing the self as an illusion appears to be untenable since one must presuppose knowledge of reality in order to distinguish the self from self as an illusion. To assert the self is "not real" assumes knowledge of what *is* real, something Hindus claim is unknowable (cf. *Upanishads*). Reincarnation is criticized for offering no objectively verifiable data by which to defend the doctrine. Human souls are said to have no beginning and are eternal (which implies a temporal existence without change), but an inconsistency emerges when one discovers that a change of consciousness is required to be released from the cycle of reincarnation.	The inherent difficulty with the doctrine of denying the reality of self is how one can deny one's own self while existing and not existing simultaneously. The denial of self assumes knowledge of what is real (reality), something many Buddhists claim does not exist. To declare that nothing really exists when people are experiencing evil and suffering is not only disheartening, it appears to favor a pessimistic view of life offering a subtle temptation to suicide and/or to diminish the desire for philanthropic service.
Sin/Evil	Sin or evil has no objective reality, but is a social construct. Moral relativism is the sober truth—morality is just a human idea that differs from one culture to another.	The god Shiva is the source of good and evil. Evil is chaos, suffering, destruction, or bondage. Sin is moral or ritual and is defined as bad karma.	The root of all evil is ignorance and desire (attachment). The presence of evil and suffering in the world is viewed as evidence against the existence of God.
Objections	Assailants view the rejection of absolutes as contradictory since it is an absolute belief/statement to deny absolutes. Plus there seem to be certain absolutes that the majority hold true, such as freedom, right to life, air, food, and water, and the right to free speech. Most also believe certain actions, such as the killing of innocents, to be absolutely wrong. If morals are merely a social construct rooted in culture, how are moral conflicts between cultures resolved? There must be something above culture to adjudicate moral problems.	Since sin or evil is understood in terms of karmic debt that must be worked off, it implies that some moral discernment by another is required to ensure the proper amount of debt has been charged to the individual. Discernment calls for an evaluation process which in turn requires an omniscient mind to take into account all deeds performed by individuals. Who or what is the moral arbiter? Some assert that karma is deterministic in nature since what one does in this life determines one's condition in this life or the next. Evil and suffering may continue indefinitely since any remedy is from imperfect human beings.	Critics have rejected the notion of ignorance and desire as being the root of evil since they fail to account for how a lack or gain of knowledge and awareness results in evil. For there are ignorant persons who have desire and yet do not appear to be evil. Alternatively, there are those who appear to have great knowledge and awareness and commit evil. Many see Buddhism as failing to make a distinction between knowledge and goodness, and between all desire and "misplaced" desire. Some have questioned how this ignorance has come upon mankind and been transmitted from person to person. Buddhist arguments against God's existence because of suffering seem unfounded since it presupposes future knowledge that evil will *never* be overcome. According to Christianity, evil has been overcome spiritually and judicially, but is yet to be overcome practically.

Chart 38

World Religions (continued)

Topic	Secular Humanism	Hinduism	Buddhism
Salvation	Since humanism denies the existence of a spiritual problem within man (sin nature) along with denial of a supernatural deity, there is no supernatural or spiritual salvation as such. Humanistic "salvation" resides within mankind and is defined in terms of overcoming ignorance through education and achieving personal and global progress. Yet humans are eternal in the sense that after death, the body becomes "one with the universe" and is scattered throughout. There is no "afterlife" as such.	Brahman seeks to save/liberate all mankind. Salvation consists of escaping (liberation, or *moksha*) the endless cycles of birth, death, and rebirth (reincarnation) by eliminating karmic debt and realizing that "Atman is Brahman" and entering into the presence of Brahman.	The achievement of salvation is hindered by ignorance. Nirvana can be achieved via meditation. The *Eightfold Path* focuses on such elements as wisdom, conduct or social order, and meditation to achieve nirvana, the point at which the self realizes the nonexistence of the self, thus discovering permanence.
Objections	Secular Humanists attempt to "save" society/mankind by curing its ills through education and awareness. Critics point out that to *know* what is good through education is not the same as to accomplish the good. History has demonstrated (Hitler, Stalin) that knowledge is no guarantee that individuals will act morally or in the best interests of society. The Secular Humanists' denial of the afterlife is unnecessary since the mind (logic), being immaterial, can be fully functional even when the body, being material, is not functional. There is no reason to reject that the immaterial mind is somewhat independent of the physical body, making it at least possible that the mind could exist beyond the death of the body. That is to say, if the mind exists immaterially and independent of the body, why couldn't it exist in similar fashion after the death of the body? Christians often refer to the evidence supporting the resurrection of Jesus Christ in particular in order to support the belief in the afterlife in general.	Within the Hindu doctrine of an unchanging ultimate reality emerges an inherent conflict with the mode of salvation that is reflected in the crucial question: How can an individual, who is ignorant of his real identity as the unchanging Brahman, change in consciousness in the process of self–realization, or, more precisely, how can the unchanging change?	Though meditation is the primary vehicle through which nirvana is achieved, some challenge it as being inadequate. The critical question is: Why rely on a changing, deluded, suffering being to liberate itself from attachment and the delusion it finds itself in? What confidence does one have to gain a proper evaluation of one's current situation of a world that is an illusion? If Buddhism is correct, then nothing is better than something, which some say is not possible because nothing has *nothing* to compare. The argument has been made that personal existence with the presence of some evil is a superior mode of being to that of no existence and no evil present.
Time	Time is conceived as finite (Einstein's General Theory of Relativity), woven into the fabric of the universe along with space and matter.	Just as the universe is without beginning, so too is time.	Time is eternal (or at least potentially infinite).

Chart 38

World Religions (continued)

Topic	Secular Humanism	Hinduism	Buddhism
Objections	Theists believe the Secular Humanist view of time as finite suggests that the temporal world had a cause at its beginning, which implies that the cause must be outside of time. Time cannot be the cause of itself since this would imply that time both existed and did not exist at the same moment. Time cannot be uncaused since this would violate the law of causality that says all finite things need a cause. Time cannot be eternal since, according to the Kalam argument (it is impossible to go backwards infinitely), it is impossible to traverse backwards an infinite amount of moments (time), yet we have arrived at today, which is the sum of the moments that went before this present time. Therefore, time must be finite, thus requiring a cause.	The Hindu view of time as everlasting (no beginning or end) is problematic due to difficulties explaining how one can cross an everlasting span of time. Time cannot be eternal since it is impossible to traverse an infinite number of moments of time, yet we have arrived at today, which is the sum of the moments that went before this present time, therefore, time must be finite—thus requiring a cause (cf. Kalam cosmological argument).	The Buddhist view of time is subject to the same criticism as the Hindu view, namely, that it is impossible to traverse an infinite series of moments because there is no beginning and no end. It is the same as trying to cross an infinite bridge—one never arrives at the end because there is no end to the bridge. To assert that time is "potentially infinite" does not solve the problem since one more moment (or in the case of the bridge, a plank) could always be added, thus never reaching the end. Yet we have reached the end (today), which is the sum total of all moments that preceded the present. Simply to assert that time continues forever does not change the *quality* of time, it only changes the *quantity* of time by stretching it out. And if time is finite as Einstein discovered, the principle of causality requires that it had a cause. The cause itself must be ontologically prior (i.e., prior in being) to the temporal universe of which time is a part.
Other Religions	The right use of reason and empirical science provides a reliable way of knowing things and discerning objective truth. Thus secular humanism is exclusivistic in that it takes itself to be true and whatever is contrary to it to be false.	In most of its forms Hinduism is a pluralistic religion, with nonexclusive modes of practice in which one can use different means (yoga, foods, psycho-physical exercise) to worship any number of deities. Mankind can approach ultimate reality in many different ways.	Teaches that there are a limited number of things to learn from other religions.
Objections	Secularists have focused on creating a separation between the realm of fact, reason, science, history, and truth and the realm of faith. However, it seems problematic to separate the two domains since spiritual significance often depends on a historical event. The meaning of salvation for Christians is inextricably linked to the historical event of Christ's death on the cross.	Philosophically Hinduism appears to be as exclusive as its competitors. That is to say, if all pluralism is true, then all non-pluralism must be false. Some contend that all religions are exclusive, with greater and lesser degrees of flexibility within the religious system itself.	Most would agree that one can learn some peripheral things from other religious perspectives. However, core tenets that characterize and define the nature of a particular religion are mutually exclusive and would appear to be contradictory to other religions.

Chart 38

World Religions (continued)

Topic	Taoism	Shinto	Confucianism
Reality	The universe is macrocosmic. The Tao (an impersonal force of existence) is the Way or Path in all reality. The Tao is present in all aspects of reality, including nature, which reveals how humans ought to morally conduct themselves.	Advocates worship of *kami* (nature spirits). The universe is spiritual in nature.	Stresses human relationships over preoccupation with the supernatural. Affirms an impersonal power called "heaven." Government should be for the good of all people.
Objections	Scholars have pointed out problematic issues with this view of reality and life. Nature may not be the best pattern for life since some creatures kill their mates after procreation (e.g., Black Widow spider) or cannibalize their offspring if threatened (e.g., hamsters, rabbits). Animals do not emulate what most societies recognize as virtuous, such as long-term relationships, accountability, stability, and moral character (animals, plants, and inanimate matter are considered amoral). Nature also does not exhibit the best characteristics in all circumstances, as when hurricanes, tornadoes, tidal waves, and earthquakes claim innocent lives due to nature's volatility, unpredictability, and instability—characteristics that are considered undesirable in human culture. At best, nature is a contributor to our actions, not a determiner or ideal model for them.	Some suggest that the *kami*, which derive their origin from other *kami*, do not deserve ultimate worship or allegiance since they are finite gods. Christians have long asserted that only an Ultimate Being deserves one's ultimate loyalty, allegiance, and worship. To do otherwise appears to be a misplaced affection. Furthermore, from Shinto emerges a mythical view of reality that describes the *kami* as creating the world through fantastical means, which presents an unevidential, unjustifiable, and unrealistic sense of reality. Obviously, myth can be a powerful medium by which to illustrate a truth, but is not appropriate to serve as the basis of truth or as the basis for the practice of a worldview. Truth corresponds to reality as it actually exists.	The Confucian view of reality has several problems. First, the preoccupation with proper etiquette and social interaction has generated a mechanistic and rigid formality seemingly unconcerned with the moral quality that lies behind the action itself. That is, is the action good because it may bring some beneficial result such as order, or is it good for its own sake? If it is the former, then the Confucian system opens the door to relativism and pragmatism, both of which have severe problems of their own. If it is the latter, which is unlikely in the Confucian system, absolutism emerges. Education as the means by which political, moral, and social change occurs appears unsatisfactory. One may know what is right and still choose to do what is wrong.
Revelation	Taoism formally became a religion in AD 440 and was considered by many to be a cult. The chief writings are the *Tao-Te-Ching* and the *Chung-Tzu*.	Earliest books are the *Kajiki* (AD 712) and *Nihonshoki* (AD 720), compiled approximately 1,300 years after the events they record in the history of early Japan.	Confucius cited four books and wrote one himself (the five classic Analects). Other texts include *The Great Learning*, *Doctrine of the Mean*, and the *Book of Mencius*.

Chart 38

World Religions (continued)

Topic	Taoism	Shinto	Confucianism
Objections	Problems emerge when the *Tao-te-ching* attempts to describe the Tao. First, the Tao is described as "beyond words" and rational thought. Yet it makes no sense to describe the Tao, as the *Tao-te-ching* does, in words if it is indescribable with words. It may be objected that the Tao is only described by what it is *not* (i.e., by way of negation or *via negativa*), not by what it actually is using positive descriptions. Despite this noble attempt to clarify the issue, it is insufficient since negative language always presupposes some positive knowledge. More precisely, one cannot say "The bicycle does not work" without *first* knowing something about the bicycle's qualities. In addition, the Tao is described as reverting to "nothingness." If it is true that the Tao undergoes substantial change to nothingness, what *cause* is posited for not only its nonexistence, but also its return to existence? The Tao's existence could not be uncaused since everything that has a beginning, or undergoes substantial change, needs a cause (cf. principle of causality). It could not be self-caused because it is impossible to be and not be simultaneously. The only remaining alternative is that the Tao was caused by someone/something else. Another problem surfaces when realizing that only temporal things change (time measures change). Therefore, if the Tao changed, it is finite and in need of a cause. And if an infinite regress of causes is impossible, as the Kalam cosmological argument suggests, the Tao is not ultimate, but rather the efficient first cause is ultimate.	The Shinto books have been criticized for presenting a mythical worldview that millions of people have adopted as the basis for their spiritual and secular life. The works do not claim any kind of divine inspiration and should not be considered infallible in spiritual or historical matters. Questions have been raised as to the veracity and reliability of the ancient books because of the enormous time gap between events (the mythological beginnings of Japan) and the written word.	Some suggest that Confucian literature gives an incomplete message, focusing only on a system of ethics and social conduct and virtually ignoring the afterlife and the vertical relationships between God(s) and man. However, it can be argued that Confucius never intended to start a religion or even to encourage any kind of worship or ritual any different from the status quo.
God	"God" is an impersonal force.	The most important deities are Vjigami, ancestral deities of particular Uji clans, and the *kami* (nature spirits).	Affirms the existence of a supernatural being, T'ien. In later Confucianism heaven is believed to be an impersonal force.

Chart 38

World Religions (continued)

Topic	Taoism	Shinto	Confucianism
Objections	Since "God" is described as an impersonal force of existence, and at times beyond existence (i.e., nonexistence), several criticisms have been identified. First, an impersonal God seems too distant and detached from human affairs. Thus, it is questionable as to whether the Taoist worldview should be adopted. A God that cannot relate to human needs cannot offer comfort, praise, or blame to individuals. Second, some have questioned the logical consistency of the Tao. It is impossible for a nonbeing to exist or even to cause being. Either the Tao is, or it is not. According to the law of non-contradiction, which states that something cannot both be and not be at the same time and in the same sense, the Tao cannot both be and not be.	The concept that it is necessary for the individual to please the *kami* since the *kami* has the power for healing or harm leads to a crucial liability in Shinto, namely, the practitioner may become immersed in an atmosphere of worship that seeks only to gain an intended result instead of genuine worship for the sake of the deity itself. If one seeks only practical value in worship, that worship will be easily replaced when something better arises. The deities appear to be capricious and arbitrary since they do not possess a nature that prohibits them from doing evil one day and good the next.	Confucian thought has been criticized for lacking a foundation on which to ground ethical behavior and being. Before Confucius was born, Chinese religion described a personal spirit, Shang ti, that ruled the upper spirit realm. Confucius appears to speak of this reality as an impersonal heaven called T'ien. Heaven's function seems to be the ground of creativity for the whole universe.
Mankind	Humans live and function as part of nature. One can understand the nature and behavior of humans through an adequate grasp of the universe.	Humans are part of the spiritual universe in which they exist.	Teaches that humans are morally neutral and can be swayed by strong leaders. Seeks to perfect mankind via wisdom and morality. Stresses the centrality of human relationships.
Objections	Some believe that the teaching that people align themselves with the Tao through "purposeful inactivity" (*wu-wei*), or, more precisely, by remaining in a posture of nonaggressive behavior by doing what is natural and spontaneous, encourages overly passive living, which breeds complacency with one's present circumstances. Certain circumstances, such as poverty, immorality, and harmful situations, should be vigorously addressed until changed. Others have pointed out the inherent relativism present in such a view of life. Ultimately, it appears as if the Taoist view of mankind, which suggests that one should "go with the flow," allows the flow of natural circumstances to determine, or at least greatly influence, one's decisions.	The Shinto belief that newborns are either a result of *kami* giving life or a *kami* actually incarnating itself into the baby has led to the claim that Japan as a whole and its people in particular are divine. Their belief in the afterlife appears to take various forms that reflect syncretism (combining diverse religious beliefs). The individual may return to the *kami* that gave the life originally or be remembered as an ancestor spirit which can return by being born into a family once again, even the very same family. This belief in reincarnation comes under attack from Western culture and from theistic religions.	The Confucian belief that man is inherently neutral artificially creates a category that does not exist. Man is either good *or* bad within his neutrality. Most likely Confucius (551–479 BC) and his follower Mencius (c. 371–c. 289 BC) would argue for the inherent goodness of mankind, which appears to conflict with common experience that suggests the opposite. That is to say, why do we have to teach children to be kind to one another and to tell the truth? To respond by saying the children need the right moral examples to emulate would be simply pushing the problem back one step to then examine why there are not many moral examples available. In addition, problems emerge when one attempts to explain how mankind can be influenced by and exposed to good moral behavior and patterns, yet still chooses to do evil. At best, it appears that a good moral environment with good patterns and examples to follow can only be a *contributing* cause to good behavior, not a *determining* cause.

Chart 38

World Religions (continued)

Topic	Taoism	Shinto	Confucianism
Sin/Evil	Only human intervention upsets natural events. Humans act in ways that are not natural. They strive against the Tao instead of flowing with it. Stresses virtue but holds that to seek it indicates a lack of it. "The man of superior virtue is not virtuous, and that is why he has virtue."	Sin is ritualistic and called pollution. One can become ritually polluted by contact with the dead or through sexual activity. Sinfulness is not based on strictly moral or ethical considerations.	Mankind is not evil and hence there is no significant sin problem to deal with. Training in wisdom is thought to be important. Ethics in personal relationships is crucial.
Objections	The Taoist approach to evil is the subject of criticism in at least three areas. The sweeping assertion of inaction or nonintervention without distinguishing the kind of human intervention has a tendency to reduce good actions (such as planting trees in the forest to promote a healthy environment) and to elevate evil actions (such as forest arson, which brings death and destruction) to the same quality of action, when they are clearly distinct in moral value. Balance, harmony, moderation, and "going with the flow" are not always the best path to take. Some situations—emergencies—ought to be approached with extreme measures. And even if one were to grant the assumption that evil, disorder, and chaos are overcome through "action without action" (*wu-wei*), the natural order of things does not always function this way. Finally, the belief that a man of superior virtue is not virtuous and that is why he has virtue, is an illogical statement that violates the law of noncontradiction. Also, it is illogical to assert that one has virtue when one is not virtuous. The man either has virtue or he does not.	Because Shinto offers no solution to the problem of evil, it has drawn criticism for placing an overemphasis on the here and now, living only for the moment to gain all the practical earthly benefits the *kami* have to offer. The lack of moral commands or absolutes seems to be a liability to Shinto, especially when relativism is the alternative.	The extreme focus on relationships seems to be a narrow approach since it views relationships on a superficial extrinsic level, leaving the motives, purpose, and intent of individuals largely unaddressed. Perfecting etiquette appears to foster an environment of rigid formalism without considering the individual's will. Even if the process worked and brought order, it is possible to have an orderly immoral society or culture. Most believe that a moral society that lacks etiquette and order is much better than an orderly society with immoral characters.
Salvation	To become "one with Tao" is the Way or Path.	To be granted protection and good fortune by the Kami, one must go through ritual purification before worshiping the Kami.	Salvation is viewed in terms of bringing order to this world through creating harmony between humanity and nature. Self-examination results in being true to one's own inner nature and applying that insight to one's relationships with others.

Chart 38

World Religions (continued)

Topic	Taoism	Shinto	Confucianism
Objections	The concept of yielding to one's circumstances with no intention of changing those circumstances (*wu-wei*) should not be an absolute rule since some people do find themselves in harmful circumstances, as when one is in the path of an oncoming train or automobile. It also is not clear how one becomes "one" with the Tao. If it means "identity to nature," it falls prey to the same criticism that plagues pantheism. Namely, a switch from nonidentity to identity implies change of either consciousness or being, and all change implies temporality, which the Taoist and the pantheist are not willing to admit within the ultimate eternal reality. If it means be *harmonious* with nature, most would agree that a proper relationship to the natural world is essential for self-preservation.	The Shinto system offers little or no motivation for living a moral life that has benefits beyond this world. The lack of rewards and punishments appears inequitable since evil committed in this life remains unpunished and good goes unrewarded.	Confucian emphasis on education as critical to fostering proper relationships with others in the family and society cannot guarantee a moral or orderly society. To know what is good and orderly is not the same as doing what is good and orderly.
Time	Cyclical view of time and history.	Time is potentially infinite.	Time is potentially infinite.
Objections to View	There appears to be no objective evidence for the contention that time and history are cyclical. The subjective testimonies of former lives have been shown to be false or unverifiable.	Some have challenged the potentially infinite view of time by suggesting that a "potential infinite" is really a finite since it will never really be actualized, but remains in a state of potentiality. Therefore, if time is finite and since no potential can actualize itself, time needed a cause that is infinite and atemporal (non-temporal). There must have been an infinite eternal actualizer of time and the finite temporal world.	The Confucian view of time is subject to the same criticisms as Taoism and Shinto. No evidence that time and history are cyclical or that the view of time as potentially infinite is possible, suggesting instead that a "potential infinite" is a finite since it will remain in a state of potentiality that is never actualized. Since no potential can actualize itself, time needed a cause, an infinite eternal actualizer.
Other Religions	The Tao alone is the Way.	Shinto does not espouse rigid beliefs. However, it maintains that Japan is the only divine land and that its people are divine.	Has mixed fairly well with various forms of Buddhism and Taoism. It has fundamental differences with much of Western thought, however.
Objections	Taoists view favorably only those religions and individuals that demonstrate a greater degree of social, political, and moral order while simultaneously advocating a simple lifestyle.	Shinto's belief that Japan and its people are the only divine land and group in the world tends to foster a sense of superiority and power in relationship to other religions.	Confucianism's view of theistic religions, especially Christianity, possesses significant differences. While Confucian religion agrees regarding the end (relational order), it differs as to the means by which to achieve that end. Confucianism stresses an epistemological solution, while theism posits a moral solution.

Sources:
Winfried Corduan, *Neighboring Faiths: A Christian Introduction to World Religions* (Downers Grove, Ill.: InterVarsity Press, 1998).
Norman L. Geisler, *Baker's Encyclopedia of Christian Apologetics* (Grand Rapids: Baker, 1999).
David Noebel, *Understanding the Times: Religious Worldviews of Our Day and the Search for Truth* (Eugene, Ore.: Harvest House, 1994).

Chart 38

Secular Humanism versus Christianity

Secular Humanism	Issue	Christianity
Big bang by natural causes, or eternal universe	Origin	Creation by God
Socrates, Marx, Freud, Huxley	Thinkers/Writers	Jesus, Moses, Paul, Augustine
Grecian/European Chinese	Cultural Base	Hebraic
Mankind	Authority	God, the Bible
Know and please self	Purpose in Life	Know and love God and all people
Rejected	God	Worshiped
Animal elevated by chance	Man	Created as *imago Dei*, in the image of God
Result of chance without purpose	Universe	Special creation to glorify God
Relative	Truth	Absolute
Superstitious book by humans	Bible	Revelation of God
Ultimately anarchy or big government/socialism	Government	Freedom under God
Accepted as individual's right to personal freedom	Abortion	Not allowed, viewed as causing death to an unborn child
Stresses experimentation, autonomy, and sexual freedom	Sexual Purity	Good in the context of monogamous marriage
Emphasis on rights	Children	Emphasis on responsibility
Acceptable due to birth/choice	Homosexuality	Abomination to God

Chart 39

PART 5
BIBLICAL
APOLOGETICS

Old Testament Manuscripts

Name	Original Date of Composition[1]	Date of Earliest Copy	Books
Dead Sea Scrolls	15th or 13th to 4th century BC	250 BC–AD 68	Includes 223-plus biblical manuscripts from every book of the Hebrew Bible except Esther
Dead Sea Isaiah Scroll (1QIs-a)	8th century BC	150–100 BC	Only complete Hebrew copy of the entire book of Isaiah
Dead Sea Scroll 1 Samuel (4Q Samuel-B)	10th to 9th century BC	4th to 3rd century BC	Contains 1 Samuel 16, 19, 21, 23 Perhaps the oldest Dead Sea manuscript to date
Rylands Papyrus 458	15th or 13th century BC	150 BC	Contains Greek portions of Deuteronomy 23–28
Nash Papyrus	15th or 13th century BC	150 BC–AD 68	Damaged portion of the Decalogue Exodus 20; Deuteronomy 5:6–21; Shema 6:4-9
Peshitta	15th or 13th to 4th century BC	AD 100–200	Entire Old Testament in Syriac
Chester Beatty Papyri	15th or 13th to 8th century BC	AD 150	Contains large portions of Genesis, Numbers, Deuteronomy, Isaiah, Jeremiah, Daniel, Esther, and Ecclesiastes
Targum of Onkelos	15th or 13th century BC	AD 200	Torah
Codex Vaticanus (B)	15th or 13th to 4th century BC	AD 325	The Old Testament and Apocrypha in Greek uncial except portions of Genesis, 2 Kings, Psalms, 1 and 2 Maccabees, and the Prayer of Manesses
Codex Ephraemi Rescriptus	13th to 10th centuries BC	AD 345	Contains Job, Proverbs, Ecclesiastes, Song of Solomon
Codex Sinaiticus (ℵ)	13th to 4th centuries BC	AD 350	Half of the Old Testament in Greek uncial

Chart 40

Latin Vulgate	AD 390–405	Entire Old Testament in Latin
Codex Alexandrinus (A)	13th to 4th centuries BC	AD 450	Entire Old Testament in Greek uncial
British Museum Oriental 4445	13th century BC	AD 850	Pentateuch
Codex Cairensis (C)	13th to 4th centuries BC	AD 895	Former and latter prophets
Aleppo Codex	13th to 4th centuries BC	AD 900	Oldest complete Hebrew text of the Old Testament
Leningrad Codex	8th to 4th centuries BC	AD 916	Isaiah, Jeremiah, Ezekiel
Codex Leningradensis B-19A (L)	13th to 4th centuries BC	AD 1008	Complete Hebrew text of the Old Testament
Samaritan Pentateuch (SP)	13th century BC	10th to 11th centuries AD	Pentateuch written in Samaritan characters

[1] Whether the books of Moses were composed in the 15th century BC or the 13th century BC depends on how one views the date of the exodus, as late 15th century or early 13th century BC. Most conservative scholars embrace the earlier date, thus around 1440 BC for composition of the Pentateuch, while some conservative scholars and most liberal scholars prefer the early 13th century BC for its composition.

Chart 40

Old Testament Archaeology

Name	Date	Archaeological Evidence
Adam and Eve Seal	3500 BC	The Sumerian seal found by E. A. Speiser depicts a naked man and woman bowed in humiliation being driven out, followed by the serpent (Genesis 3:23).
Amarna Tablets	1400 BC	In 1887 a peasant woman stumbled across clay tablets with cuneiform inscriptions. Subsequent deciphering revealed the early conquests of Canaan by the Hebrews known by the name "Habiru." The tablets, in conjunction with other discoveries at Mari and Nuzi, confirm that the Habiru were well known in Mesopotamia by the early second millennium BC.
Babylonian Chronicles	600 BC	The chronicles report on King Nebuchadnezzar's first decade as king. Information pertaining to his political and military exploits have been published since 1954, but of special interest are the details of Nebuchadnezzar's invasion of Palestine in the late 7th and early 6th centuries BC, which corresponds to the prophecies of Jeremiah, 2 Chronicles 36:9, and 2 Kings 24.
Behistun Inscription	500 BC	Monument inscription refers to the Persian victory over Babylon and the rise of Darius I (522–486 BC) to power (Daniel 5:31; 6:1; Nehemiah 12:22; Ezra 4-6; Haggai 1:1, 15; 2:10).
Belshazzar Inscription (Nabonidus Chronicle)	6th century BC	For years historians denied the historical existence of "Belshazzar." Then in 1854 Henry Rawlinson discovered an inscription in Ur that named "Bel-shar-usur" (Belshazzar) as the eldest son and coregent with King Nabonidus, who was often away from Babylon and left Belshazzar as king. This clarifies Daniel 5:29, which says that Daniel was the "third ruler in the kingdom."
Black Obelisk of Shalmanaser III	841 BC	Discovered in 1846 by A. H. Layard in the palace of Nimrud, the Black Obelisk confirms the historical personage and military victories of the Assyrian king (and biblical figure) Shalmaneser III. In addition, the obelisk portrays Israel's King "Jehu, son of Omri" bowing to pay tribute before Shalmaneser (2 Kings 9–10).
Code of Hammurabi	1765-1700 BC	Historians have long asserted that the Israelites were too primitive to have such an advanced Mosaic law code by the 15th century BC. Instead they place Israel's law formulation in the 5th or 6th century BC. However, with the discovery of Hammurabi's sophisticated code (282 laws dealing with morality, commerce, and religion), which predates Mosaic Law, there is little question as to the possibility of a 15th century BC chronology of the Mosaic Law. Moreover, the Hammurabi Code, which predates Moses by more than 200 years, answers the objection that writing was a much later development in Canaan.
Cyrus Cylinder	500 BC	Persian clay cylinder discovered by Hormuzd Rassam that chronicles Cyrus's victory and the issuing of his decree permitting freedom of worship and the return of captives with their gods to their own land (cf. Ezra 1:1–3; 6:3–5; Isaiah 45:1).
Ebla Tablets	2350 BC	This remarkable discovery by Paolo Matthiae while excavating Tell Mardikh, south of Aleppo, Syria, yielded approximately 16,000 clay tablets that describe various cities such as Sodom, Zeboim, Hazor, Megiddo, Jerusalem, and Gaza, which were previously thought to be legendary. In addition, the tablets reveal names that bore resemblance to the Hebrew names used 200 years later, such as Nahor, Israel, Michael, Ishmael, and Eber. Several deities named Dagon and Baal are identified, which correlates to the biblical narrative.

Chart 41

Old Testament Archaeology (continued)

Gilgamesh Epic	2000 BC	Babylonian clay tablets that describe a flood that possesses remarkable similarities to the flood recorded in the book of Genesis. The god Ea warns Utnapishtim to build a square ship in which to endure the week-long deluge. After the storm, the waters subside in one day. The deities are saddened over the destruction and make a covenant with Utnapishtim and grant him divine immortality. Though there are notable differences, it is consistent with a record that would be established after such a great event. Worldwide there are more than thirty separate accounts of the flood from various people groups.
Goliath Inscription	10th–9th centuries BC	During excavations at Tell es-Safi (Gath, in southern Israel) in 2005, a pottery shard with archaic proto-Canaanite letters was discovered to be an inscription which contained wording remarkably similar to the biblical name of Goliath (1 Samuel 17). The discovery means that names similar to or identical with Goliath were in use at the time the biblical narrative records the confrontation between the biblical characters David and Goliath.
Hittites	1300 BC	Once thought to be mythological due to the lack of extra-biblical mention, the Hittites proved to be historical when A. H. Sayce (in 1876) and Hugo Winckler (in 1906) discovered a Hittite library in central Turkey which consisted of law codes, legends, covenants, and myths. These discoveries not only establish the historicity of the kingdom, they give an understanding of Abraham's rationale for buying a portion of the land associated with the purchase of the cave of Machpelah from Ephron the Hittite (Genesis 23; 1 Kings 10:29).
House of Yahweh Ostracon	800 BC (artifact is still topic of debate among scholars)	The ostracon is a clay pottery shard used as a receipt for the donation of silver to Solomon's temple. It is the earliest piece of evidence referencing the temple outside the biblical text.
Karnak Inscription	9th century BC	Also known as the "Shishak Relief," depicts Egyptian Pharaoh Shishak's military victories over Rehoboam in the late 10th century BC. This relief corresponds to the events mentioned in 1 Kings 14 and 2 Chronicles 12.
Merneptah Stele	1230 BC	Egyptian hieroglyphic slab containing Pharaoh Merneptah's military exploits and the earliest mention of "Israel" outside the Old Testament, thereby demonstrating that the ancient Israelites had inhabited Canaan in the middle of the 13th century BC.
Moabite Stone	840–820 BC	This Moabite slab was found in 1868, east of the Dead Sea, by F. A. Klein. It documents the military conflict between King Mesha and the Israelites. It records the name "Yaweh" and how Omri, king of Israel, defeated Moab only to allow Omri's son Ahab to rule the land. Eventually, after one generation, the god Chemosh enabled Mesha to reoccupy the land. This stone establishes the historicity of Omri, the usage of "Yaweh," and the biblical accounts in 2 Kings 1:1; 3:4–5.
Nuzi Tablets	1500–1400 BC	Excavations at Nuzi, in modern Iraq, led to the discovery of thousands of clay tablets, written in a Babylonian dialect, that describe important parallels in law, customs, and society with the biblical patriarchs as late as the first millennium BC. One set of documents reveals that if a man did not have a son, he may adopt a slave, relative, or freeborn man to care for the elder man and carry on his name. This is reminiscent of Abraham's relationship with Eliezer in Genesis 15:2–4. Other documents illuminate a custom for women who, unable to conceive, gave their husbands another wife to bear children to become the family heir (Genesis 16:2). If in the future the first wife bears children, the second wife and her son would be given a share of the family wealth and could not be cast out. Perhaps this explains why Abraham was reluctant to expel Hagar and Ishmael (Genesis 21:10–11).

Chart 41

Old Testament Archaeology (continued)

Siloam Inscription	700 BC	In 1880, archaeologists discovered a cursive Hebrew inscription at the southern end of Hezekiah's 1,700-foot limestone water tunnel. It tells of how two groups of workers tunneled from the Pool of Siloam to a retention pool inside the Jerusalem city walls (2 Kings 20:20; Isaiah 22:9ff; 2 Chronicles 32:30–31).
Tayler Prism	701 BC	The six-sided clay prism found in 1830 at Nineveh records the campaigns of Sennacherib (705–681 BC) against Judah and Hezekiah at Jerusalem as described in Isaiah 36–37 and 2 Kings 18–19.
Tel Dan Inscription	9th century BC	In 1993 Tell Dan excavators in the area of northern Galilee near Mount Hermon unearthed a stone slab which contained several lines of incomplete Aramaic inscriptions. Among the identifiable inscriptions were the first extra-biblical citations of King David, which read, "The House of David" and "The King of Israel." Later discoveries also mention Jehoram and Ahaziah, names that correspond to 2 Kings 8–9.
Temptation Seal	3rd millennium BC	This seal, discovered in Sumer, shows the same sequence of events that occurred in the garden of Eden during the temptation of Eve. The artifact depicts a man and a woman, both seated, viewing a tree, with a serpent whispering in the ear of the woman as both are reaching for the fruit of the tree. In the past, the temptation incident was dismissed as Jewish myth. However, this seal demonstrates that the essentials of the temptation account in Genesis were well known thousands of years prior to the writing of the book of Genesis.
Weld-Blundell Prism	2100 BC	This collection of tablets offers extensive lists of Sumerian kings who reigned before and after the "great flood." The kings listed before the flood are identified with extremely long lives, whereas the kings who reigned after the flood have significantly shorter life spans, a feature consistent with the biblical account in the book of Genesis.
Yehuchal Bulla	7th–6th centuries BC	The seal (bulla), which measures only 0.4 inch wide, was discovered during excavation at the alleged site of David's palace south of the southern steps of the Temple Mount. The inscription reads: "Belonging to Yehuchal (Jehucal) ben (son of) Shelemiyahu ben Shovi," which corresponds to the person mentioned in Jeremiah 37:3; 38:1, who appears to be the courtier of King Zedekiah sent to the prophet Jeremiah.

Chart 41

New Testament Manuscripts

Name	Books	Original Date of Autograph	Earliest Date of Copy	Gap from Original
John Rylands Fragment (P52)	Selection of the gospel of John, includes John 18:31–33, 37–38 and is considered the oldest New Testament fragment known.	AD 85–100	AD 125	25–40 years
Chester Beatty Papyri (P45, 46, 47)	Contains portions of Matthew, Mark, Luke, John, Pauline epistles, and the book of Revelation.	AD 50–100	AD 200–300	100–250 years
Bodmer Papyri (P66, 72, 75)	Substantial portions of the gospel of John and the earliest copy of 1 and 2 Peter and Jude.	AD 50–70	AD 175–250	105–200 years
Codex Vaticanus (B)	Contains most of the Greek Old Testament and the majority of the New Testament.	AD 50–100	AD 325	225–275 years
Codex Sinaiticus (a)	Earliest copy of a complete New Testament except for several verses: Mark 16 and John 7 and 8. Also includes over half the Greek Old Testament (Septuagint, LXX).	AD 50–100	AD 350	250–300 years
Codex Alexandrinus (A)	Written in uncial Greek script, Alexandrinus possesses the entire Old Testament and most of the New.	AD 50–100	5th century AD	350–400 years
Codex Ephraemi (C)	Ephraemi was erased in the 12th century and then restored by Constantine Tischendorf in the 19th century. It contains portions of every book in the New Testament except 2 Thessalonians and 2 John.	AD 50–100	AD 450	350–400 years
Codex Bezae (D)	The manuscript is a rare Greek and Latin bilingual text of portions of the Gospels, Acts, and 3 John 11–15; 3 John is in Latin only.	AD 50–65	5th–6th centuries AD	400–500 years
Magdalen Papyrus	Small fragment of Matthew 26:7–8, 10, 14–15. German scholar Carsten Thiede argued for middle to late 1st century. If correct, the fragment would be the oldest manuscript of the New Testament.	AD 40–65	AD 75–200	10–160 years
Codex Claramontanus (D2)	Bilingual Greek/Latin manuscript of the Pauline Epistles, including Hebrews.	AD 50–64	6th century AD	500 years
Codex Washingtonianus	Contains the four Gospels.	AD 50–100	4th–5th centuries AD	250–400 years

Chart 42

Comparison of New Testament with Other Ancient Works

Author	Literary Works	Date	Earliest Copy	Gap from Original	Copies
Plato	*Dialogues*	4th century BC	AD 900	c. 1,250 years	20
Homer	*Iliad*	9th century BC	400 BC	c. 500 years	643
Herodotus	*The Histories*	484–425 BC	AD 900	c. 1,350 years	8
Aristotle	Assorted works	4th century BC	AD 1100	c. 1,400 years	5
Thucydides	*History of the Peloponnesian Wars*	460–400 BC	AD 900	c. 1,300 years	8
Aristophanes	Assorted works	448–385 BC	AD 900	c. 1,300 years	10
Sophocles	Assorted works	496–406? BC	AD 1000	c. 1,400 years	193
Julius Caesar	*The Gallic Wars*	58–44 BC	AD 900	c. 950 years	10
Tacitus	*Annals*	AD 58–120	AD 1100	c. 1,000 years	20
Pliny (Younger)	*History of Rome*	AD 62–113	AD 850	c. 750 years	7
Suetonius	*The Twelve Caesars*	AD 70–140?	AD 950	c. 900 years	8
				Total Other Ancient Works	**932**
Apostles and Companions	**Greek New Testament manuscripts**	**AD 45–100**	**AD 125–325**	**30–300 years**	**5,600+**
	Non–Greek New Testament manuscripts				**19,200+**
				Total New Testament manuscripts	**25, 000+**

Chart 43

New Testament Archaeology

Name	Date	Archaeological Evidence
James Ossuary (still under debate)	AD 63	The 20-inch-long limestone box is believed to have been the repository for the bones of James, brother of Jesus. The side panel of the box contains Aramaic script which reads, "James, son of Joseph, brother of Jesus." The ossuary is questioned by Israeli Antiquities, but is viewed as authentic by many scholars in the area of paleography, geology, and epigraphy. If authentic, the ossuary would be the earliest archaeological evidence directly relating to James and Jesus.
Other Ossuaries	AD 40–50	Several burial ossuaries near Jerusalem were found with the mark of the cross and various prayers directed to Jesus. They indicate early recognition that the followers of Jesus viewed his death on the cross as significant and that Jesus was God.
Meggido Church	3rd–4th centuries AD	While excavating a new compound at the Megiddo Prison in northern Israel, workers discovered an ancient church which dates to the 3rd or 4th century. This is perhaps the oldest church yet unearthed in Israel. In addition to the well-preserved mosaic floor with fish inlays, inscriptions were found which read: "The God-loving Aketous has offered this table to the God Jesus Christ as a Memorial … Gaianus … Roman military officer,… having sought honor, from his own money has made the mosaic." This find lends support to the notion that Jesus Christ was considered God by his early followers, Christianity was well-established in Israel, and Christianity appealed to various classes of society. The fact that the church was destroyed argues strongly for a third-century date since the Edict of Toleration protecting freedom of worship was issued by Rome in the early fourth century.
Nazareth Inscription	31 BC–AD 54	An inscription discovered in 1878 forbidding the robbing of tombs, originating between the time of Augustus Caesar and Claudius Caesar and found at Nazareth.[1] Since Nazareth was such a small village, scholars have conjectured that the edict may be in response to the rumor passed on by authorities in Israel regarding the robbing of the grave of Jesus, but there is no certainty attaching the inscription to the resurrection of Jesus the Messiah.
Pilate Inscription	1st century	Antonio Frova discovered a stone slab at Caesarea Maritima with a Latin inscription stating, "Tiberium Pontius Pilate Prefect of Judea." This is the only archaeological evidence giving Pilate's name and title.
Gabbatha	1st century	According to William F. Albright, the court location of Jesus' trial that is identified in John 19:13 and Matthew 27:27 as "the Pavement" or "Gabbatha" is believed to be at the Roman military headquarters (Tower of Antonia) in Jerusalem, located at the northwest corner of the temple area.
Gallio Inscription	1st century	In 1908, an inscription was found in northern Greece (Delphi) that identifies "Gallio" as "Proconsul" being in office from AD 51–53, which corresponds to Luke's record in Acts 18:12–14.

Chart 44

Zeus and Hermes	1st century	In 1909, archaeologists unearthed several inscriptions and a temple near Lystra that identified Zeus and Hermes as the two most important gods, since they were believed to have visited the earth. These gods were expected to return in the future, which helps scholars understand the reaction of the people when trying to identify Barnabas and Paul as Zeus and Hermes (Acts 14:6–13).
The Erastus Inscription	1st century	This inscription, found at Corinth in 1929, identifies a city official as the one who built the pavement where the inscription lies, dated around AD 50. He is probably the Erastus of Romans 16:23. The inscription, in typical abbreviation, is ERASTUS PRO:AEDILIT E: S:P:STRAVIT, and translated by John McRay as "Erastus, curator of public buildings, laid (this pavement) at his own expense." The term "aedile" referred to one in charge of the financial matters of the city.
Yohanan Crucifixion	1st century	Crucifixion victim Yohanan Ben Ha'galgol was discovered in 1968 in northeastern Jerusalem. Researchers gained vital information about crucifixion practices in the middle 1st century that corroborate Christ's crucifixion experience as described in the Gospels. They discovered that Ben Ha'galgol was crucified with seven-inch spikes driven through the feet and lower arm. In addition, both legs were broken (Ps. 22; Matt. 27; Mark 15; Luke 23; John 19).
Pool of Bethesda	1st century	During excavation in 1888 near the Church of St. Anne, the remains of the Pool of Bethesda mentioned in John 5:2 were discovered. Previously this pool had no extra-biblical mention.
Pool of Siloam	Late 1st century BC—early 1st century AD	In June 2004 the 1st-century pool of Siloam was discovered near what had traditionally been called the pool of Siloam (dating to the 5th century AD). The newly found pool, at the bottom of Hezekiah's tunnel at the foot of the city of David, is much larger than the Byzantine pool. This pool is mentioned in John 9 as the site of the healing of a blind man who was told by Jesus to wash the mud from his face to receive his sight.
Coins	1st century	Various coinage spoken of in the New Testament, such as silver shekels (Matthew 26:14–15), tribute penny (Mark 12:13–17), and the widow's mite (Luke 21:1–4), have been identified as historical.

[1] Arguing for a date under Claudius around AD 50, see Jack Finegan, *Light from the Ancient Past: The Archaeological Background of the Hebrew-Christian Religion*, Vol. II (Princeton, N.J.: Princeton University Press, 1959), 299, while an early date in the time of Octavius Augustus Caesar is argued by M. Franz Cumont, "Un Rescrit Impérial sur la Violation de Sépulture," *Revue Historique* (January–April 1930): 241–66.

Chart 44

Archaeologists and Historians Confirm Biblical Reliability

Sir Fredrick Kenyon	"The interval then between the dates of original composition and the earliest extant evidence becomes so small as to be in fact negligible, and the last foundation for any doubt that the Scriptures have come down to us substantially as they were written has now been removed. Both the *authenticity* and the *general integrity* of the books of the New Testament may be regarded as finally established"—Sir Frederic Kenyon, *Bible and Archaeology* (London: Harrap, 1940), 288–89.
A. N. Sherwin-White	"For Acts the confirmation of historicity is overwhelming. Yet Acts is, in simple terms and judged externally, no less of a propaganda narrative than the Gospels, liable to similar distortions. But any attempt to reject its basic historicity even in matters of detail must now appear absurd. Roman historians have long taken it for granted"—A. N. Sherwin-White, *Roman Law and Roman Society in the New Testament* (Grand Rapids: Baker, 1963), 189.
Nelson Glueck	"It may be stated categorically that no archaeological discovery has ever controverted a biblical reference. Scores of archaeological findings have been made which confirm in clear outline or exact detail historical statements in the Bible"—Nelson Glueck, *Rivers in the Desert: A History of the Negev* (New York: Farrar, Strauss & Cudahy, 1959), 31.
Sir William Ramsey	"Luke is a historian of the first rank; not merely are his statements of fact trustworthy ... this author should be placed along with the very greatest of historians"—William Ramsey, *The Bearing of Recent Discovery on the Trustworthiness of the New Testament* (Grand Rapids: Baker, 1953), 222.
William F. Albright	"Aside from a few die-hards among older scholars, there is scarcely a single biblical historian who has not been impressed by the rapid accumulation of data supporting the substantial historicity of the patriarchal tradition"—William F. Albright, *The Biblical Period from Abraham to Ezra* (New York: Harper & Row, 1960), 2.
Edwin M. Yamauchi	"Until the breakthrough of archaeological discoveries, the stories about the biblical patriarchs—Abraham, Isaac, and Jacob—were subject to considerable skepticism.... In the last thirty years, however, a steadily increasing flow of materials from Mesopotamia and Syria-Palestine—from Mari, from Nuzi, from Alalakh—has convinced all except a few holdovers, of the authenticity of the patriarchal narratives"—Edwin M. Yamauchi, *The Stones and the Scriptures* (Philadelphia and New York: J. B. Lippincott, 1972), 36.
Millar Burrows	"The excessive skepticism of many liberal theologians stems not from a careful evaluation of the available data, but from an enormous predisposition against the supernatural"—Millar Burrows, *What Mean These Stones?* (New York: Meridian, 1956), 176. "The Bible is supported by archaeological evidence again and again. On the whole, there can be no question that the results of excavation have increased the respect of scholars for the Bible as a collection of historical documents. The confirmation is both general and specific"—Millar Burrows, "How Archaeology Helps the Student of the Bible," in *Workers with Youth* (April 1948): 6, as cited in Josh McDowell, *New Evidence That Demands a Verdict* (Nashville: Thomas Nelson, 1999), 100.
Joseph P. Free	"In addition to illuminating the Bible, archaeology has confirmed countless pages which have been rejected by critics as unhistorical or contradictory to known facts"—Joseph P. Free, *Archaeology and Bible History* (Wheaton, Ill.: Scripture Press, 1969), 1.

Chart 45

Jewish and Pagan Historians Confirm Biblical History

Name	Source	Date	Statement	Comment
Flavius Josephus	*Jewish Antiquities* 18.63–64	AD 93	"About this time arose Jesus, a wise man (if indeed it be right to call him a man). For he was a doer of marvelous deeds, and a teacher of men who gladly receive the truth. He drew to himself many persons, both of the Jews and also the Gentiles. (He was the Christ.) And when Pilate, upon the indictment of leading men among us, had condemned him to the cross, those who had loved him at the first did not cease to do so (for he appeared to them alive on the third day—the godly prophets having foretold these and ten thousand other things about him). And even to this day the race of Christians, who are named from him, has not died out."	This statement, often called the *Testimonium Flavianum*, has some phrases which are suspect as being from Josephus since they would appear to be representative of one who embraced Jesus as the Messiah. At present there is considerable debate on the seemingly Christian inclusions.
Flavius Josephus	*Jewish Antiquities* 20.200	AD 93	"He [Annas the younger] convened a judicial session of the Sanhedrin and brought before it the brother of Jesus the so-called Christ—James by name—and some others, whom he charged with breaking the law and handed over to be stoned to death."	Appears to be an unaltered and genuine statement.
Babylonian Talmud	*Sanhedrin* 43a	Originally AD 70–200 compiled later in Talmud	"Jesus was hanged on Passover Eve. Forty days previously the herald had cried, 'He is being led out for stoning, because he practiced sorcery and led Israel astray and enticed them into apostasy. Whosoever has anything to say in his defence, let him come and declare it.' As nothing was brought forward in his defence, he was hanged on Passover Eve."	It is significant that the charge against Jesus was concerning the religious law of Israel rather than Roman law.
	Sanhedrin 43a	Originally AD 70–200 compiled later in Talmud	"[Rabbi] Ulla said, 'Would you believe that any defence would have been so zealously sought for him? He was a deceiver, and the All Merciful says: "You shall not spare him, neither shall you conceal him." It was different with Jesus, for he was near to the kingship.'"	A Jewish apologetic note against Christians may be present here. "Near to the kingship" is a reference to his descent from David.
	Sanhedrin 43a	Originally AD 70–200 compiled later in Talmud	"The rabbis taught: Jesus had five disciples: Mathai, Naqai, Nezer, Buni and Todah."	This has little historical value. Mathai may be Matthew, Todah perhaps is Thaddaeus, Naqai conceivably is Nicodemus, Buni may be a form of Boanerges, and Nezer may relate to Nazarene.

Chart 46

Jewish and Pagan Historians Confirm Biblical History (continued)

Pliny (the Younger)	*Epistles* 10.96 "Letter to Trajan"	AD 110	"[Christians] maintained ... that their fault or error amounted to nothing more than this: they were in the habit of meeting 'on a certain fixed day before sunrise and reciting an antiphonal hymn to Christ as God, and binding themselves with an oath—not to commit any crime, but to abstain from all acts of theft, robbery and adultery, from breaches of faith, from repudiating a trust when called upon to honor it. After this ... it was their custom to separate, and then meet again to partake of food ... '"	The letter is too lengthy to produce in full. Pliny as legate of Bithynia wrote Trajan concerning how to deal with the rapid growth of Christians in his area.
Tacitus	*Annals* 15.44	AD 115–117	"But all human effort, all the lavish gifts of the emperor, and the propitiations of gods, did not banish the sinister belief that the conflagration was the result of an order. Consequently to get rid of the report, Nero fastened the guilt and inflicted the most exquisite tortures on a class hated for their abominations, called Christians by the populace. Christus, from whom the name had its origin, suffered the extreme penalty during the reign of Tiberius at the hand of one of our procurators, Pontius Pilate, and a deadly superstition, thus checked for the moment, again broke out not only in Judaea, the first source of the evil, but also in the City, where all things hideous and shameful from every part of the world meet and become popular."	Tacitus records several features which are consistent with the New Testament, that Christianity gained the name from Christ, Christianity reached Rome, Christ's death occurred during the reign of Tiberius, Jesus was put to death by Pontius Pilate, Christianity began in Judaea, and that Christians were despised and persecuted.
Mara bar Serapion	Syriac manuscript in British Museum	c. AD 73–300	"What advantage did the Athenians gain from putting Socrates to death? Famine and plague came upon them as a judgment for their crime. What advantage did the men of Samos gain from burning Pythagoras? In a moment their land was covered with sand. What advantage did the Jews gain from executing their wise King? It was just after that that their kingdom was abolished. God justly avenged these three wise men: the Athenians died of hunger; the Samians were overwhelmed by the sea; the Jews, ruined and driven from their land, live in complete dispersion. But Socrates did not die for good; he lived on in the statue of Hera. Nor did the wise King die for good; he lived on in the teachings which he had given."	The writer was probably not a Christian or he would have said that Jesus rose from the dead. He simply places Jesus on a par with other wise men of antiquity. He was most likely influenced by Christians, since he blames the Jews rather than the Romans for the execution of Jesus.
Suetonius	*Life of Claudius*	AD 120	"He expelled the Jews from Rome, on account of the riots in which they were constantly indulging, at the instigation of Chrestus."	Chrestus was a popular misspelling of the Greek Christos. Suetonius apparently misunderstood the police records, thinking that Chrestus was in Rome and a ringleader of the riots in AD 49.
Suetonius	*Life of Nero*	AD 120	"Punishment was inflicted on the Christians, a body of people addicted to a novel and mischievous superstition."	This statement refers to the persecution by Nero c. AD 64.

The basis for this chart comes primarily from F. F. Bruce, *Jesus and Christian Origins Outside the New Testament* (Grand Rapids: Eerdmans, 1974); additional information is from Bruce M. Metzger, *The New Testament: Its Background, Growth and Content* (New York: Abingdon, 1965). Adapted by permission.

Chart 46

Jesus in the Writings of Paul

Paul's View of Jesus	Evidence from Paul's Writings
Jesus the Messiah is Lord and God	• **Paul described Jesus as God** • God forever praised (Romans 9:5) • Shared the nature of God (Philippians 2:6) • Yahweh, before whom all will bow (Philippians 2:11) • Son of God (Romans 1:3–4) • Great God and Savior (Titus 2:13)
The exalted Christ and the historical Jesus are the same	• **The exalted Jesus is the Jesus of Nazareth** • He was an Israelite (Romans 9:5; Galatians 3:16) • He was of the tribe of David (Romans 1:3) • He lived under the law (Galatians 4:4) • He had a brother by the name of James (Galatians 1:19) • He was poor (2 Corinthians 8:9) • He ministered among the Jews (Romans 15:8) • He had twelve disciples (1 Corinthians 15:5) • He instituted a Last Supper (1 Corinthians 11:23–25) • He was crucified, buried, and raised again in his physical body (1 Corinthians 1:23; Galatians 3:1, 13; 2 Corinthians 13:4; 1 Corinthians 15:4) • **Paul knew traditions about Jesus' character** • His meekness and gentleness (2 Corinthians 10:1) • His obedience to God (Romans 5:19) • His endurance (2 Thessalonians 3:5) • His grace (2 Corinthians 8:9) • His love (Romans 8:35) • His total humility and obedience (Philippians 2:6–8) • His righteousness (Romans 5:18) • His sinlessness (2 Corinthians 5:21) • **Paul quotes sayings of Jesus** • Marriage and divorce (1 Corinthians 7:10–16 based on Mark 10:10–12) • Right of gospel preachers to have material needs met (1 Corinthians 9:14 and 1 Timothy 5:18 based on Luke 10:7) • Words used at the institution of the Lord's Supper (1 Corinthians 11:24–25 based on Matthew 26:26–29; Mark 14:22–25; Luke 22:14–23) • **Paul bases his teaching on the teachings of Christ** • Romans 12:1–15:7 based on Matthew 5–7 • 2 Corinthians 10:1 based on Matthew 11:29 • Romans 15:3, "even Christ did not please Himself" • Romans 15:1 based on Mark 8:34 • Philippians 2:7 based on Luke 22:27; John 13:4–17

Chart 47

Historical Christological Heresies

Viewpoints	Ebionites	Docetists	Arians
Proponents	Judaizers	Basilides Valentinus Patripassians Sabellians	Arius, presbyter of Alexandria Origen (?)
Time	2nd century	Late 1st century	4th century
Denial	Genuine deity	Genuine humanity	Genuine deity
Explanation	Christ had the Spirit after his baptism; he was not preexistent	Jesus appeared human but was really divine	Christ was the first and highest created being; semi-Arians argued for *homoiousia* (like the essence of the Father) rather than *homoousia* (same as the essence of the Father)
Condemned	No official condemnation	No official condemnation	Council of Nicea, AD 325
Associated with	Legalism	Evil of the material world and oussian divinity as taught by Marcion and Gnosticism	Generation=creation
Argument for	Monotheistic	Affirmed Christ's deity	Taught that Christ is subordinate to the Father
Argument against	Only a divine Christ is worthy of worship (John 1:1; 20:28; Hebrews 13:8)	If Christ were not human, He could not redeem humanity (Hebrews 2:14; 1 John 4:1–3)	Only a divine Christ is worthy of worship; this view tends toward polytheism. Only a divine Christ can save (Philippians 2:6; Revelation 1:8)
Major Opponents	Irenaeus Hippolytus Origen Eusebius	Irenaeus Hippolytus	Athanasius Ossius

Chart 48

Historical Christological Heresies (continued)

Viewpoints	Appollinarians	Nestorians	Eutychians
Proponents	Appollinarius, bishop of Laodicea Justin Martyr	Represented by Nestorius, 5th-century bishop of Constantinople	Represented by Eutychius Theodosius II
Time	4th century	5th century	5th century
Denial	Completeness of humanity	Unity of person	Distinction of natures
Explanation	The divine Logos took the place of the human mind. Jesus was neither human nor divine—a *tertium quid* (third thing)	Union was moral, not organic—thus two persons. The human was completely controlled by the divine	Monophysitist; the human nature was swallowed by the divine to create a new third nature—a *tertium quid* (third thing)
Condemned	Council of Antioch, AD 378, 379 Council of Constantinople, AD 381	Synod of Ephesus, AD 431	Council of Chalcedon, AD 405 Defended by "Robber Synod" of Ephesus, AD 449 Condemned by Chalcedon, AD 451
Associated with	Logos=reason in all people	"Word-flesh" (Antiochene) not "word-man" (Alexandrian) Christology; opposed to using *theotokos* (i.e., God-bearer) of Mary	Concern for the unity and divinity of Christ; Alexandrian (minimized humanity)
Argument for	Affirmed Christ's deity and real humanness	Distinguished human Jesus, who died, from Divine Son, who cannot die	Maintained the unity of Christ's person
Argument against	If Christ did not have a human mind, He would not be truly human (Hebrews 2:14; 1 John 4:1–3)	If the death of Jesus was the act of a human person, not of God, it could not be efficacious (Revelation 1:12-18)	If Christ were neither a man nor God, He could not redeem as man or as God (Philippians 2:6)
Major Opponents	Vitalis Pope Damascus Basil Theodosius Gregory of Nazianzus Gregory of Nyssa	Cyril of Alexandria	Flavian of Constantinople Pope Leo Theodoret Eusebius of Dorylaeum

Chart 48

False Views of the Two Natures of Christ

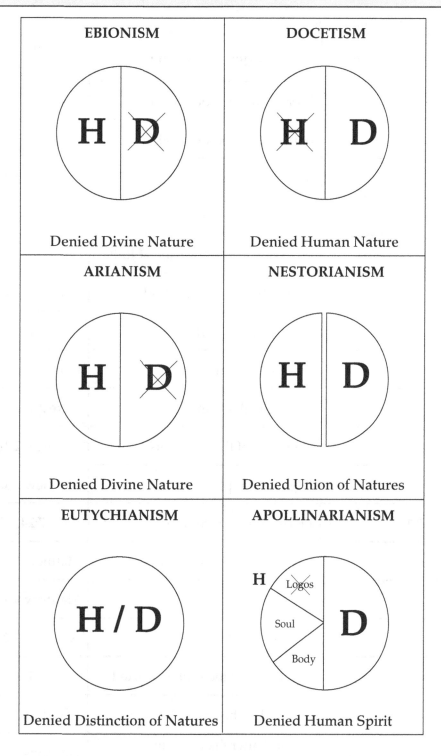

EBIONISM

Denied Divine Nature

DOCETISM

Denied Human Nature

ARIANISM

Denied Divine Nature

NESTORIANISM

Denied Union of Natures

EUTYCHIANISM

Denied Distinction of Natures

APOLLINARIANISM

Denied Human Spirit

Chart 49

Messianic Prophecies Fulfilled in Christ

Presented in the Order of Their Fulfillment

Scripture Stating Prophecy	Subject of Prophecy	Scripture Stating Fulfillment
Genesis 3:15	Born of the seed of a woman	Galatians 4:4
Genesis 12:2–3	Born of the seed of Abraham	Matthew 1:1
Genesis 17:19	Born of the seed of Isaac	Matthew 1:2
Numbers 24:17	Born of the seed of Jacob	Matthew 1:2
Genesis 49:10	Descended from the tribe of Judah	Luke 3:33
Isaiah 9:7	Heir to the throne of David	Luke 1:32–33
Daniel 9:25	Time for Jesus' birth	Luke 2:1–2
Isaiah 7:14	Born of a virgin	Luke 1:26–27, 30–31
Micah 5:2	Born in Bethlehem	Luke 2:4–7
Jeremiah 31:15	Slaughter of the innocents	Matthew 2:16–18
Hosea 11:1	Flight to Egypt	Matthew 2:14–15
Isaiah 40:3–5; Malachi 3:1	Preceded by a forerunner	Luke 7:24, 27
Psalm 2:7	Declared the Son of God	Matthew 3:16–17
Isaiah 9:1–2	Galilean ministry	Matthew 4:13–17
Deuteronomy 18:15	The prophet to come	Acts 3:20, 22
Isaiah 61:1–2	Came to heal the brokenhearted	Luke 4:18–19
Isaiah 53:3	Rejected by his own (the Jews)	John 1:11
Psalm 110:4	A priest after the order of Melchizedek	Hebrews 5:5–6
Zechariah 9:9	Triumphal entry	Mark 11:7, 9, 11
Psalm 41:9	Betrayed by a friend	Luke 22:47–48
Zechariah 11:12–13	Sold for thirty pieces of silver	Matthew 26:15; 27:5–7

Chart 50

Messianic Prophecies Fulfilled in Christ (continued)

Psalm 35:11	Accused by false witness	Mark 14:57–58
Isaiah 53:7	Silent to accusations	Mark 15:4–5
Isaiah 50:6	Spat upon and smitten	Matthew 26:67
Psalm 35:19	Hated without reason	John 15:24–25
Isaiah 53:5	Vicarious sacrifice	Romans 5:6, 8
Isaiah 53:12	Crucified with transgressors	Mark 15:27–28
Zechariah 12:10	Body pierced	John 20:27
Psalm 22:7–8	Scorned and mocked	Luke 23:35–36
Psalm 69:21	Given vinegar and gall	Matthew 27:34
Psalm 109:4	Prayer for his enemies	Luke 23:34
Psalm 22:18	Soldiers gambled for his coat	Matthew 27:35
Psalm 34:20	No bones broken	John 19:32–33, 36
Zechariah 12:10	Side pierced	John 19:34
Isaiah 53:9	Buried with the rich	Matthew 27:57–60
Psalm 16:10; 49:15	Would rise from the dead	Mark 16:6–7
Psalm 68:18	Would ascend to God's right hand	Mark 16:19

Chart 50

Introduction to the Jesus Seminar

Proponents	Fellows of the Jesus Seminar come from various academic, professional, and religious backgrounds that include Protestants, Jews, Catholics, atheists, professors, one pastor, some unidentified, and a film maker. Among the approximately 70 scholars and laypersons that comprise this group, several influential members have emerged in the public awareness. These include Robert W. Funk (co-chair), John Dominic Crossan (co-chair), Marcus Borg (Oregon State University), and Paul Verhoeven (film producer).
Founding	The Jesus Seminar was initially founded in the early 1980s by the editorial board (Robert W. Funk, John Dominic Crossan, Burton Mack, and Robert Tannehill) of *Foundations & Facets*, a series published by Fortress Press. Currently the Seminar operates under the auspices of the Westar Institute based in Sonoma, California, and is sponsored by Polebridge Press. The institute functions as a theological think-tank which publishes its own research in *Foundations & Facets Forum*.
Purpose and Publications	The fellows of the Jesus Seminar meet annually to make pronouncements regarding their various research projects. The primary aim is the "conception and execution of research and publication projects connected with the Jesus tradition. … In connection with this work, the JESUS SEMINAR will create new instruments and tools and explore new and modified methodologies." One recent project evaluated 1,500 sayings of Christ in the Gospels and published the conclusions in *The Five Gospels: What Did Jesus Really Say?* Other publications include Borg, *Jesus in Contemporary Scholarship*; Funk, *Honest to Jesus*; and Crossan, *The Essential Jesus*; *The Historical Jesus*.
Approach to Biblical Studies	The Jesus Seminar rejects the following: • The inerrancy of the Bible • The deity of Christ • The miracles recorded in Scripture • The guilty until proven innocent model • The relatedness of religious faith and history The Jesus Seminar accepts the following: • Negative critical scholarship • Jesus as Galilean sage, revolutionary, or peasant • Anti-supernaturalism • Historical skepticism and revisionism historians use to evaluate ancient literature • The bifurcation of faith and history
Philosophical Assumptions	First is the acceptance of anti-supernaturalism, or the rejection of miracles. Scientific discoveries of Charles Darwin and Galileo require that scholars understand the universe as "secular" rather than conforming to the dogmatic pronouncements of earlier church creeds and councils. That is, the real Jesus will be discovered through historical investigation rather than through theological formulas. Faith and reason are viewed as separate domains which are mutually exclusive. The supernatural reflects the domain of faith; science is the domain of reason.
Methodological Assumptions	"Seven Pillars of Scholarly Wisdom" guide the methodology while researching the sayings of Jesus.[1] These include: 1. Distinguishing between the "Jesus of history" and the "Christ of Faith"; 2. The gospels of Matthew, Mark, and Luke are closer to the historical Jesus than is the gospel of John; 3. Mark was the first gospel to be written and serves as the basis for both Matthew and Luke; 4. The hypothetical source Q (*Quelle*) is given as the explanation for the common material found in Matthew and Luke but not found in Mark; 5. The liberation of the non-eschatological Jesus from the eschatological Jesus of Albert Schweitzer; 6. The distinction between Jesus' oral culture and our modern print culture, implying that authentic Jesus sayings are short, memorable, provocative sentences and stories; 7. The burden of proof is upon those who declare the Gospels to be historical since they are now assumed to be embellished by myth.
View of Jesus	Jesus is viewed in two distinct ways: first, there is the "Jesus of history," the one who critical scholars are searching for and who is unlike the gospel portrayal of him as a supernatural divine figure that raises the dead, redeems man, and calls for saving faith. It is believed that early followers, church creeds, and councils foisted upon Jesus mythical embellishments that wrongfully elevated him to divine status. Second, the "Christ of faith" is described as the Jesus who is worshiped as God in many churches today. According to the Seminar, this Jesus is not an accurate representation of the "real" Jesus of history. Jesus, in some sense, needs to be liberated "from the scriptural and creedal and experiential prisons" in which he has been kept.[2]

[1] Robert W. Funk, Roy W. Hoover et al., *The Five Gospels: What Did Jesus Really Say?* (New York: Macmillan, 1993), 2–5.
[2] Ibid.

Chart 51

Evaluation of the Jesus Seminar

Category	Critical Evaluation
Proponents	First, the Jesus Seminar's claim that it offers a "scholarly consensus" on their projects as a result of approximately 70 scholars is misleading, since over half of the 6,900 members of the Society of Biblical Literature and thousands of others who have scholarly training were not involved in Seminar research. Second, though there were a few members from Canada and South Africa, the Seminar is mostly composed of North American scholarship. The absence of British and conservative participation in the studies precluded facing any challenging peer review. Third, most of the members did not hold a distinguished academic position and were considered the more "radical" proponents in Jesus scholarship. Also, most major universities, seminaries, and graduate schools were not represented.
Founding	During the initial founding, those connected with the original *Foundations & Facets* publication were invited to become charter fellows of the Seminar. Their ranks quickly swelled to about 200 before shrinking to about 70 in the early 1990s. When the nature, scope, and methodology of their work became clear, several fellows quit the project.
Purpose and Publications	The general aim and conclusions of the group have come under considerable criticism due to the unusual nature of their "new" methods and tools. Despite these criticisms, Seminar publications continue to be widely read, not necessarily because of new evidence, but because of novel approach leading to unorthodox conclusions.
Approach to Biblical Studies	The Seminar's approach to biblical studies appears to be symptomatic of its reliance on Enlightenment ideas that seek to elevate human reason as the final and paramount criterion for truth and its uncritical acceptance of the Enlightenment's anti-supernaturalism. The bifurcation between religious faith and history has created a chasm that has separated facts from values, when in fact the two domains are inextricably linked. For the Christian, the importance of history's link to faith holds a prominent role, since to deny the historical nature of crucial events such as the crucifixion and resurrection is essentially to deny the spiritual significance and effect—Christianity cannot be real without the historical events. It is also problematic to separate facts and values on a social/moral level, since moral and immoral actions extend to historical events/facts (e.g., murder). And though there can be a distinction between the two domains, it appears problematic to posit a radical dichotomy.
Philosophical Assumptions	Most prominent among the Seminar's philosophical assumptions is the insistence that modern scientific discoveries have dismantled the supernatural worldview of times past. There are several problems with eliminating miracles in favor of scientism. First, if science is the test for truth and rationality, certain realities such as the laws of logic, values, freedom, and virtue would be considered obsolete and anachronistic, since they do not fit within the confines of scientific observable testability. Second, science relies on certain principles to engage in the scientific endeavor—such as honesty, nobility, and knowledge—which themselves cannot be tested by science. Third, the laws of nature are no longer assumed to be fixed in unalterable rigid patterns; rather, they can be described as flexible descriptions of how the universe *generally* operates and not how it *necessarily* operates. Finally, whatever occurs in the natural world can have a supernatural source beyond the world.

Chart 52

Evaluation of the Jesus Seminar (continued)

Category	Critical Evaluation
Methodological Assumptions	The Seven Pillars of Scholarly Wisdom pose several problems: (1) This separation unnecessarily detaches Jesus from the realm of fact (history); hence, any Jesus that is discovered with faith characteristics is automatically eliminated from consideration. (2) To eliminate the gospel of John due to its portrayal of Jesus as "spiritual" is unfounded and necessarily excludes, prior to evaluating the evidence, any Jesus that is nonsecular. Further, secondary differences do not determine historicity. (3) It is possible that Mark serves as a source for Matthew and Luke. (4) **Q** may not exist; dissimilarity can be accounted for in other ways due to diversity of theological purpose and audience. (5) This pillar was established in the 1970s and '80s prior to any review of the evidence and deliberations concerning the sayings of Christ. Antisupernatural bias limits their view of an eschatological Jesus. (6) This pillar wrongfully assumes that 1st-century culture was not able to preserve large quantities of material from memory, when in fact just the opposite is the case. (7) Historians have long held that ancient documents are presumed innocent until proven guilty by statements contrary to fact or internal contradictions.
View of Jesus	It appears that the Seminar initiated its research with the assumption that the historical Jesus ought to be separated from the Jesus worshiped by faith. However, how can one come to this conclusion before the research has been conducted? The Christological bifurcation at the outset of the study necessarily ensures that the only kind of Jesus that will be discovered is a finite, natural, and fallible man denuded of any divine attributes and completely detached from the realm of fact. As such, it is not difficult to understand how the Jesus Seminar determined that 82% of the gospel sayings of Jesus are inauthentic.

Response based on Joseph M. Holden, *An Examination and Evaluation of the Jesus Seminar* (unpublished master's thesis, 1997), Southern Evangelical Seminary.

Chart 52

Jesus Seminar and the Bible

Jesus Seminar	Orthodox Christianity
• *Post*-Enlightenment view of the Bible.	• *Pre*-Enlightenment view of the Bible.
• Bible is a *natural* book.	• Bible is a *supernatural* revelation.
• Investigation *determines* revelation.	• Investigation *discovers* revelation.
• Bible is mythically embellished.	• Bible is historical.
• Bible is guilty until proven innocent.	• Bible is innocent until proven guilty.
• Rejects what the Bible says about itself.	• Accepts what the Bible says about itself.
• Biblical miracles do not occur and are considered violations of the laws of nature.	• Biblical miracles are real and are exceptions to the laws of nature.
• Gospels are separated from history.	• Gospels are based in history.
• Bible has been redacted (meaning changed).	• Bible has been edited (no change of meaning).
• Synoptic Gospels written AD 70–90.	• Synoptic Gospels written AD 45–68.
• *Man* is the efficient and instrumental cause of the Bible.	• *God* is the efficient cause and *man* is the instrumental cause of the Bible.
• If the Bible is inspired, the interpreter must be inspired.	• Can have fallible interpretation of a divinely inspired revelation.
• If inerrancy was true, we would have the originals.	• Inerrancy is possible without the originals since we have good copies.
• Reject New Testament reliability because of the great span of time between Christ's death and the writing of the Synoptic Gospels after AD 70.	• Accept New Testament reliability because of the close proximity of time from the death of Christ to the writing of the Synoptic Gospels in the mid-1st century.
• The Synoptic Gospels (Matthew, Mark, Luke) are closer to the historical Jesus than the gospel of John.	• All the Gospels accurately reflect Jesus.
• Similarities in the words used prove the gospel writers were dependent on a common source.	• Thematic similarities are expected when writers are reporting the same events.
• Gospel of Thomas is an early Christian document.	• Gospel of Thomas is a Gnostic document.
• **Q** (*quelle* = source) is a source to help explain the content and similarities common to Matthew and Luke which are not found in Mark.	• **Q** (*quelle* = source) is a questionable source. It is not necessary to explain the composition of the Gospels. Similarities can be accounted for due to reporting the same events. Differences are due to each writer's unique theological purpose.

Chart 53

Critics' Views of the "Jesus of History" and the "Christ of Faith"

Jesus of History (The Jesus who really lived)	Christ of Faith (The Jesus "invented" by the church)
• Historically accurate figure	• Mythically embellished figure
• Galilean sage or peasant	• Divinely incarnated Son of God
• Natural figure	• Supernatural figure
• Revered and respected	• Worshiped
• Characterized by fact	• Characterized by faith
• This figure is discovered	• This figure is determined
• Discovered through historical investigation	• Determined through creedal formulation
• Not the proper object of faith	• Proper object of faith
• Figure that is liberated from myth, since myths are erroneous	• Figure that is imprisoned to myth because of those who developed Jesus as the Christ of faith
• Possesses an actual biological father	• Born of the Virgin Mary
• Non-eschatological figure	• Eschatological figure
• Rarely contained in the Bible (Jesus' words are considered fabrications and distortions of the early church)	• Full revelation of Christ in the Bible
• Emphasizes social and cultural change	• Emphasizes spiritual and relational change
• Revolutionary	• Redeemer
• Crucified and buried for punishment	• Crucified, buried, and resurrected for sin
• Spoke of intrinsic rewards and punishments	• Both intrinsic/extrinsic rewards and punishments
• Figure described in critical scholarship	• Figure described in the Nicene Creed
• Pre- and post-Easter Jesus are different	• Pre- and post-Easter Jesus are identical
• Figure is finite, mortal, corporeal, human	• Figure possesses both deity and humanity
• Only Jesus of Nazareth	• Both Jesus of Nazareth and Jesus Christ

Adapted from Joseph M. Holden, *An Examination and Evaluation of the Jesus Seminar* (unpublished master's thesis, 1997), Southern Evangelical Seminary.

Chart 54

Theories on the Resurrection of Jesus Christ

I. Occupied Tomb Theories

Theory	Explanation	Refutation
Unknown Tomb Charles A. Guignebert	The body of Jesus was buried in a common pit grave unknown to His disciples. Therefore, the resurrection account arose out of the ignorance as to the whereabouts of the body.	1. Not all criminals were buried in a common pit. 2. The New Testament gives Joseph of Arimathea as a witness to the burial in a specific family tomb. 3. The women saw the body being prepared for burial and knew the tomb's location. 4. The Romans knew where the tomb was, for they stationed a guard there.
Wrong Tomb Kirsopp Lake	The women came to the wrong tomb, for there were many similar tombs in Jerusalem. They found an open tomb and a young man who denied that this was Jesus' tomb. The frightened women mistakenly identified the man as an angel and fled.	1. The women did not come looking for an open tomb, but for a sealed one. They would surely bypass the open tomb if they were unsure of the exact location of the correct tomb. 2. The man at the tomb not only said, "He is not here," but also, "He is risen." 3. The women had noted the tomb's location seventy-two hours earlier. 4. The Jews, Romans, and Joseph of Arimathea knew the location of the tomb and could easily have identified it as proof against any resurrection.
Legend Early Form Critics 18th and 19th centuries	The resurrection was a fabrication to meet the church's needs that evolved over a lengthy period to vindicate a leader long since dead.	1. Recent historical criticism has shown that the resurrection stories are of mid–1st century origin. 2. Paul, in 1 Corinthians (AD 55), speaks of the resurrection as a fact and points to 500 eyewitnesses, many of whom were still alive for anyone to question.
Spiritual Resurrection Gnostics Jehovah's Witnesses	Jesus' spirit was resurrected, though His body remained dead.	1. This denies the Jewish understanding of resurrection (bodily, not spiritually). 2. Christ ate and was touched and handled. 3. To prove the resurrection false, the Jews could have shown the occupied tomb to their fellow Jews.
Hallucination Agnostics	The disciples and followers of Jesus were so emotionally involved with Jesus' messianic expectation that their minds projected hallucinations of the risen Lord.	1. Could more than 500 people, in different situations, with differing degrees of commitment to Jesus, with different understandings of Jesus' teachings, all have had hallucinations? 2. Many appearances occurred to more than one person. Such simultaneous illusions are unlikely. 3. The disciples were not expecting Christ's resurrection. They viewed His death as final. 4. The Jews could have pointed to the occupied tomb to prove them false.

Chart 55

Theories on the Resurrection of Jesus Christ (continued)

II. Unoccupied Tomb Theories

Theory	Description	Response
Passover Plot Hugh Schönfield	Jesus planned to fulfill the Old Testament prophecies of both suffering servant and ruling king through a mock death and resurrection. Joseph of Arimathea and a mysterious "young man" were coconspirators. The plot went bad when the soldier speared Jesus, who later died. The "risen Lord" was the young man.	1. The guard posted at the tomb is ignored in Schönfield's theory. 2. The basis of the theory is faulty. The resurrection myths on which Jesus supposedly based His plot were not evident until the 4th century AD. 3. Such a "resurrection" could not account for the dramatic change in the disciples. 4. All but four biblical witnesses are accounted for, especially the 500 eyewitnesses whom Paul spoke of as still living. 5. The whole plot of enduring crucifixion (and in doing so, alienating His national supporters) seems unlikely.
Resuscitation (Swoon) 18th century Rationalists	Jesus did not die on the cross; He fainted from exhaustion. The cold temperature and spices revived Him.	1. Medical science has proved that Jesus could not have survived the scourging and crucifixion.[1] 2. Could this nearly dead Jesus make an impression as the risen Lord?
Body Stolen by the Disciples Early Jewish leaders' account	The disciples stole the body while the guards were sleeping.	1. If the guards were sleeping, how did they know that the disciples stole the body? 2. Severe penalties, even death, would be imposed for sleeping on duty. The highly disciplined guards would not have slept, certainly not every single one. 3. There is no way that the disciples could possibly have overcome the guard. 4. It is preposterous to believe that the disciples died for a lie that they created.
Existential Resurrection Rudolf Bultmann	A historical resurrection will never be proved, but it is not necessary. The Christ of faith need not be bound to the historical Jesus. Rather, Christ is raised in our hearts.	1. The early disciples were convinced by historical events, observable phenomena, not on wishful thinking or hallucination or theory. They based their faith on what they saw and what they were told by the risen Jesus (Luke 24:33–53; 1 Corinthians 15:3–8).

Based on and adapted from Josh McDowell, *The Resurrection Factor* (San Bernardino, Calif.: Here's Life, 1981). Used by permission.

[1] See study in William D. Edwards, Wesley J. Gabel, and Floyd E. Hosmer, "On the Physical Death of Jesus Christ," *Journal of the American Medical Association* (March 21, 1986): 1455–63.

Chart 55

Early Church Fathers on the Nature of the Resurrection Body

Proponent	Date	Statement
Clement of Rome	AD 30–101	"There will be a future resurrection" (*The First Epistle of Clement*, 24).
Ignatius of Antioch	AD 105	"And I know that He was possessed of a body not only in His being born and crucified, but I also know He was so after His resurrection, and believe that He is so now" (*Epistle of Ignatius to the Smyrnaeans*, 3).
Tatian	AD 110–172	"And on this account we believe that there will be a resurrection of bodies after the consummation of all things; not as the stoics affirm, according to the return of certain cycles, the same things being produced and destroyed for no useful purpose, but a resurrection once for all" (*Address of Tatian to the Greeks*, 6).
Athenagoras	2nd century AD	"There must by all means be a resurrection of the bodies which are dead, or even entirely dissolved,… but it is impossible for the same men to be reconstituted unless the same bodies are restored to the same souls" (*The Resurrection of the Dead*, 25).
Justin Martyr	AD 110–165	"If the resurrection were only spiritual, it was requisite that He, in raising the dead, should show the body lying apart by itself, and the soul living apart by itself. But now He did not do so, but raised the body, confirming in it the promise of life" (*On the Resurrection, Fragments*, 9). "And when He [Jesus] had thus shown them that there is truly a resurrection of the flesh, wishing to show them this also, that it is not impossible for flesh to ascend into heaven (as he had said that our dwelling-place is in heaven), 'He was taken up into heaven while they beheld,' as He was in the flesh" (Ibid.). "The resurrection is a resurrection of the flesh which died.… It is not impossible that the flesh regenerated; and seeing that, besides all these proofs, the Saviour in the whole Gospel shows that there is salvation for the flesh" (Ibid., 10).
Clement of Alexandria	AD 195	"In the resurrection, the soul returns to the body, and both are joined to one another" (*Fragments of Clemens Alexandrinus*, 1).
Tertullian	AD 197	"We profess our belief (in public) that it [the flesh of Christ] is sitting at the right hand of the Father in heaven; and we further declare that it will come again from there in all the pomp of the Father's glory: it is therefore just as impossible for us to say that it [his flesh] is abolished, as it is for us to maintain that it was sinful" (*On the Flesh of Christ*, 26). "You will also allow that it was in the flesh that Christ was raised from the dead. For the very same body that fell in death, and which lay in the sepulcher, did rise again" (*On the Resurrection of the Flesh*, 44). "Having been crucified, He rose again the third day; (then) having ascended into the heavens, He sat at the right hand of the Father; sent instead of Himself the power of the Holy Ghost to lead such as believe; will come with glory to take the saints to the enjoyment of everlasting life and of the heavenly promises, and to condemn the wicked to everlasting fire, after the resurrection of both these classes shall have happened, together with the restoration of their flesh" (*On Prescription Against Heretics*, 13).
Theophilus	2nd century AD	"When thou shalt have put off the mortal, and put on incorruption, then shalt thou see God worthily. For God will raise thy flesh immortal with thy soul" (*Theophilus to Autolycus*, 1.7).

Chart 56

Irenaeus	AD 120–202	"Christ Jesus, the Son of God, who became incarnate for our salvation; and in the Holy Spirit, who proclaimed through the prophets the dispensations of God, and the advents, and the birth from a virgin, and the passion, and the resurrection from the dead, and the ascension into heaven in the flesh of the beloved Christ Jesus, our Lord" (*Against Heresies*, 1.10.1).
Hippolytus	AD 170–235	"He will accomplish a resurrection of all, not by transferring souls into other bodies, but by raising the bodies themselves" (*Against Plato On the Cause of the Universe*, 2).
Origen	AD c. 185–254	"With respect to the nature of the body, that the one which we now make use of in a state of meanness, and corruption, and weakness, is not a different body from that which we shall possess in incorruption, and in power, and in glory; but that the same body, when it has cast away the infirmities in which it is now entangled, shall be transmuted into a condition of glory" (*Origen De Principiis*, 3.6.6).
Athanasius	AD 293–373	"But of the resurrection of the body to immortality thereupon accomplished by Christ, the common Saviour and true Life of all, the demonstration by facts is clearer than arguments to those whose mental vision is sound" (*On the Incarnation of the Word*, 30.1).
Ambrose	AD 339–397	"For since the whole course of our life consists in the union of body and soul, and the resurrection brings with it either the reward of good works, or the punishment of wicked ones, it is necessary that the body, whose actions are weighed, rise again" (*On Belief in the Resurrection*, 2.52).
Augustine	AD 354–430	"Nor does the earthly material out of which men's mortal bodies are created ever perish; but though it may crumble into dust and ashes, or be dissolved into vapors and exhalations, though it may be transformed into substance of other bodies, or dispersed into the elements, though it should become food for beasts or men, and be changed into their flesh, it returns in a moment of time to that human soul which animated it at first, and which caused it to become man, and to live and grow" (*Enchiridion*, 88). "The world has come to the belief that the earthly body of Christ was received up into heaven. Already both the learned and unlearned have believed in the resurrection of the flesh and its ascension to heavenly places, while only a very few either of the educated or uneducated are still staggered by it" (*City of God*, 22.5).

All quotes cited are from either *The Ante-Nicene Fathers*, eds. Alexander Roberts and James Donaldson; 10 vols. (Peabody, Mass: Hendrickson, 1994), or *The Nicene and Post-Nicene Fathers*, ed. Philip Schaff (Peabody, Mass.: Hendrickson, 1994).

Chart 56

Three Modern Views of Christ's Resurrection Body

Wolfhart Pannenberg	Norman L. Geisler	Murray J. Harris
Jesus God and Man (1982)	*The Battle for the Resurrection* (1992) *In Defense of the Resurrection* (1993)	*Raised Immortal* (1985) *From Grave to Glory* (1990)
The tomb is empty.	The tomb is empty.	The tomb is empty.
The resurrection is not a historical event which could have been seen with the human eye.	The resurrected body of Jesus is historical and can be, and was, observed by the naked eye. It was *possible* to have witnessed the very resurrection event itself.	Jesus' resurrected body is "trans-historical" and cannot be the object of historical research; nor could the resurrection event have been seen by the "mortal gaze."
The resurrected Jesus cannot be seen through normal visual means in the temporal-spatial world as can other objects. Only through vision, extraordinary experience, or through metaphorical language can the body be observed.	The resurrected Jesus can be seen with the naked eye in the temporal-spatial world. No unique vision or extraordinary means are necessary.	The resurrected Jesus is not normally seen by the human eye.
The body of Jesus was a "spiritual body," not an earthly body. The "spiritual body" refers to its substance.	The resurrected body of Jesus is material and physical. The "spiritual body" refers to the body's *source*, not its *substance*.	Though the resurrected body of Jesus is "animated and guided" by the Holy Spirit, Jesus possessed a heavenly body not materially identical to His pre-resurrection body.
The gospel accounts of the resurrection appearances have legendary character.	The gospel accounts of Christ's appearances are historical in character with no legend or myth.	The Gospels are historical but describe the post-resurrectional appearances of Christ using the terms "appeared" and "disappear-red" to suggest that Jesus was invisible.
The corporeality of Jesus' resurrected body is legendary.	Jesus possessed a corporeal body both before and after resurrection. No legend is associated with Christ's body.	Occasionally, Jesus manifested Himself corporeally and is never associated with legend.
The resurrected body will be totally changed; no substantial or structural continuity with the pre-resurrection body will be present.	The resurrected body will have changes in secondary qualities (what you have), but remain the same in primary qualities (who and what you are).	Jesus occupied a different dwelling place as a result of bodily metamorphosis.
The resurrected body of Christ is different from the pre-resurrectional body without any material identity. Only historical and personal identity is present.	The resurrected body of Jesus is the same, yet with changes in it. There is a material and personal identity with the pre-resurrectional Jesus.	The resurrected body of Jesus will not have material or numerical identity with the body that died. Nevertheless, it will have personal identity as the same Jesus.

Chart 57

Which Resurrection Theory Best Fits the Facts?*

The numbers of facts listed in the middle column as *not* fitting the theory correspond to the "Facts about Christ's resurrection" in the right column. For example, the Wrong Tomb theory is contradicted by facts 5 through 12. Note that the only theory that fits all the historical facts about Christ's resurrection is the Bodily Resurrection view.		Facts about Christ's resurrection
Christ's tomb was:	**Historical facts that *do not* fit the theory**	**1.** Jesus died by crucifixion. **2.** He was buried. **3.** Jesus' death caused the disciples to despair and lose hope, believing that His life had ended.
Occupied:		**4.** The tomb was discovered to be empty just a few days later.
Unknown Tomb	Facts 4 through 12	
Wrong Tomb	Facts 5 through 12	**5.** The disciples had experiences which they believed were literal appearances of the risen Jesus.
Hallucination	Facts 5, 11, and 12	
Existential Resurrection	Facts 4, 5, 11, and 12	**6.** The disciples were transformed from doubters, afraid to identify themselves as being with Jesus, to bold proclaimers of His death and resurrection.
Twin (conspiracy)	Facts 4 and 11	
Legend	Facts 1 through 12	
Spiritual Resurrection (conspiracy)	Facts 4, 5, 11, and 12	**7.** The message of the resurrection was at the center of preaching in the early church.
Empty:		**8.** Soon after Jesus' death, this message was especially proclaimed in Jerusalem, where He had been buried.
Natural Theories		
Stolen by Disciples	Facts 5, 6, 11, and 12	**9.** As a result of this preaching, the church was born and grew.
Swooned	Facts 1 and 6	
Passover Plot (conspiracy)	Facts 5, 6, 11, and 12	**10.** Sunday became the primary day of worship.
Taken by Authorities	Facts 5 through 12	
Supernatural Theory		**11.** James, who had been a skeptic, was converted to the faith when he believed he saw the resurrected Jesus.
Bodily Resurrection	None (all facts fit this view)	**12.** A few years later, Paul was converted by an experience which he believed to be an appearance of the risen Jesus.

The "Facts about Christ's resurrection" were originally compiled by Gary Habermas. The Two left columns of this table were adapted from an analysis by Craig Hazen. Used by Permission.

Chart 58

Comparing Resurrection, Resuscitation, and Reincarnation

Resurrection	Resuscitation	Reincarnation
The body that dies is raised up from the grave and again joined with the soul/spirit.	The body that dies is raised up from the grave and again joined with the soul/spirit.	The body that dies disintegrates back into the earth, but the soul or consciousness comes back in a different body.
The body that is raised has changes in it.	The body that is raised has *no* changes in it.	The body is not raised, but the soul or consciousness is recycled into a body that may not be human.
The body/soul/spirit remains the same person yet possesses heavenly incorruption, immortality, glory, and power.	The body/soul/spirit remains the same person yet *does not* possess heavenly incorruption, immortality, glory, and power.	The consciousness is embodied into a circumstance for better or for worse depending on karmic debt. No heavenly attributes are present.
The dominating power source of the resurrected person is the Holy Spirit and cannot die again.	The power source of the person is intrinsically human and is subjected to death once again.	The power source is intrinsically human and the body will die again.
Resurrection is viewed as a promised event and is considered an asset.	Resuscitation is viewed as an unpromised, rare, special, and miraculous event that is considered an asset.	Reincarnation is understood as a necessary event that is a means of paying karmic debt and is considered a curse or liability.
Judaism, Christianity, and Islamic scripture: Daniel 12:1–3, 13 1 Corinthians 15:35–58 Koran (Qur'an), Sura 2:174; 37:144	Lazarus, John 11:38–44 Widow's son, Luke 7:11–15 Jairus's daughter, Luke 8:49–56	Hindu, Buddhist, and New Age literature
Judaism, Christianity, Islam	Possible for resuscitation to happen in any religion, with God as source.	Hinduism, Buddhism, New Age

Chart 59

The Problem of Miracles

Worldview and Epistemological Objections to Miracles	The possibility of miracles raises a variety of objections, some based on the worldview the objector brings to the evaluation, others from an epistemological perspective, and often some combination of both.
	
	1. **Worldview Objections**: A rejection of miracles based on one's view of reality.
	
	    a. *Atheism*: Those who take the view that there is no God reject the supernatural possibility regardless of any evidence. A miracle is deemed impossible because it is inconsistent with an atheistic worldview.
	
	    b. *Deism*: Miracles are rejected because of the belief that God put the laws of nature in motion and he would not intervene or violate those laws.
	
	    c. *Supernaturalism*: To those who accept the pantheistic worldview, there are no miracles because every event is supernatural and there is no distinction between the natural and the supernatural.
	
	2. **Epistemological Objections**: Miracles are rejected because it is either not reasonable to credit God with an anomalous event as a miracle or because there is insufficient evidence that a miracle occurred (Francis J. Beckwith, *David Hume's Argument Against Miracles: A Critical Analysis* [Lanham, Md.: University Press of America, 1989], 139).
	
	Some of the most influential objections have been epistemological and put forward by the rationalist Benedictus de Spinoza and the empiricist David Hume.

What is a miracle?	Francis J. Beckwith defines a miracle as "a divine intervention which occurs contrary to the regular course of nature within a significant religious context."[1]

Addressing some objections to miracles	Argument	Response
Deism	God created the world and wound it up like a clock and set it running under the laws of matter and motion, never to interfere with it again.[2]	The course of nature is really only the regular pattern of the operation of God's will (laws of nature are only descriptive and are not logical necessities). The natural law theories should not understand miracles as violations of the laws of nature. Rather, miracles are naturally impossible events. What could bring about a naturally impossible event? The personal God of theism.

Rationalism: Benedictus de Spinoza (1632–1677)	1. Miracles violate the unchangeable order of nature.
	
	2. Miracles are insufficient to prove God's existence. Absolute certainty is necessary.
		1. Objection based on the immutability of nature.
		  a) God was under no obligation to create the universe. God is free to will differently than he does and therefore the order of nature is alterable.
		
		2. Objection based on the insufficiency of miracles.
		  a) Christian apologists used miracles to prove that God has acted in the world and not as proofs for the existence of God (though they can be).
		  b) Two assumptions underlie Spinoza's objection: A proof for God's existence must be demonstratively certain; and God's existence is inferred from natural law. (There are other arguments for the existence of God.)
		  c) Having proved or presupposed God, miracles can show that Christian theism is true.
		  d) If Jesus resurrected from the dead, would we be justified in inferring a supernatural event? Yes. The resurrection so exceeds what we know of natural causes and the supernatural explanation is given immediately in the religio-historical context.

Chart 60

The Problem of Miracles (continued)

Empiricism: David Hume (1711–1776)	Hume attacks the possibility of the identification of a miracle. He states, "So that, upon the whole, we may conclude, that the Christian Religion not only was at first attended with miracles, but even at this day cannot be believed by any reasonable person without one. Mere reason is insufficient to convince us of its veracity: And whoever is moved by Faith to assent to it, is conscious of a continued miracle in his own person, which subverts all the principles of his understanding, and gives him a determination to believe what is most contrary to custom and experience.[3]
	
	1. "In Principle" Argument: The miracle is always weighed against the unchangeable laws of nature.
	
	2. "In Fact" Arguments: The evidence is so poor it does not amount to even a probability. Hume had four reasons:
	
	  a) Miracles are not attested to by enough educated and honest men.
	
	  b) People crave the miraculous and will believe absurd stories.
	
	  c) Miracles occur only among barbarous men.
	
	  d) Miracles occur in all religions and thus cancel each other out.
		1. The "In Principle" Argument: It is either question begging or confused. To say that the evidence for miracles must be weighed against the unchangeable laws of nature is to implicitly assume already that miracles have never occurred or could never be proved. With this type of reasoning, if a miracle did in fact occur, no evidence would be sufficient because the miraculous event would always have to be weighed against the alleged unchangeable laws of nature. Hume seems to have confused the realm of science and history.
		
		2. The "In Fact" Arguments: His four points have force, but they cannot be used to decide the historicity of any particular miracle. They only serve to make us cautious as we investigate miracles. When the evidence is evaluated, the New Testament documents turn out to be a reliable source of history. There is plenty of internal and external evidence found in the New Testament that supports its claim to the miraculous. For example, the apostle Paul was a highly educated person who became a converted skeptic based on the evidence and eyewitness testimony of Jesus' resurrection. This alone seems to address Hume's criticisms. Moreover, the miracle of the resurrection of Jesus from the dead and the evidence for the occurrence cannot be rejected out of hand because of miraculous claims by other religions. Each miracle needs to be examined on its own merit.

[1] Francis J. Beckwith, *David Hume's Argument Against Miracles: A Critical Analysis* (Lanham, Md.: University Press of America, 1989), 139.

[2] Some of this information comes from the chapter "The Problem of Miracles" in William Lane Craig, *Reasonable Faith: Christian Truth and Apologetics,* rev. ed. (Wheaton, Ill.: Crossway, 1994), 126–55.

[3] David Hume, *Enquiries Concerning Human Understanding and Concerning the Principles of Morals,* 1777, 3rd ed. reprinted with introduction and analytical index by L. A. Selby-Bigge, with text revised and notes by P. H. Nidditch (Oxford: Oxford University Press, 1975), 131.

Recommended Reading

Beckwith, Francis J. *David Hume's Argument Against Miracles: A Critical Analysis.* Lanham, Md.: University Press of America, 1989.

Brown, Colin. *Miracles and the Critical Mind.* Grand Rapids: Eerdmans, 1984.

Craig, William Lane. *Reasonable Faith: Christian Truth and Apologetics.* Revised edition. Wheaton, Ill.: Crossway, 1994.

Geivett, R. Douglas, and Gary R. Habermas, eds. *In Defense of Miracles: A Comprehensive Case for God's Action in History.* Downers Grove, Ill.: InterVarsity Press, 1997.

Lewis, C. S., *Miracles.* New York: Macmillan, 1960.

Chart 60

PART 6
SCIENTIFIC
APOLOGETICS

Main Views on the Origin of Life and of the Universe

	Naturalistic Evolution	Deistic Evolution	Theistic Evolution	Progressive Creation	Young Earth Creation
Origin of Life and the Universe; Divine Involvement	The universe was not created. It is either eternal or, if it did come into existence, it came from nothing. Inherent processes within nature produced all that exists, including man. Atoms, time, motion, and chance have formed all that is in the universe. At higher levels of life, a natural process called "natural selection" is at work. In each species, the most adaptive and strongest survive. Therefore, the species have upgraded themselves. Mutations occur within the species and a few have been helpful in this competitive struggle. These helpful mutations form the basis for new species. Man is thus far the end result of natural selection and positive mutations. There is no God; hence, there is no divine involvement.	The universe was created by God out of nothing. The world is finite, and it operates by natural laws that God set in motion. These laws are representative of God's character: eternal, perfect, immutable, orderly, and consistent. One of these laws is the law of evolution. After God created the first matter, He programmed the process of evolution. Then He withdrew from involvement within the world. He is the direct Creator only of the first living form and the indirect Creator of all else. Except for God's involvement in the beginning, deistic evolution is the same as naturalistic evolution.	God created the universe and directly created the first living form. He established the process of evolution. In this view, mutations and natural selection are God's method for producing His creation. God created matter in such a way that it has to evolve. However, God also has had involvement in the evolutionary process at specific times, intervening to modify the process. God created the first human being by using an already existing being (one of the higher primates) and giving it a human soul.	God created the universe and all that is in it directly. However, He did this at several points in time, separated by large time spans. When He brought new life forms into existence, He did not use existing matter; He created each from nothing. However, between these acts of creation, development took place within the species through the process of evolution (microevolution). God made man directly and completely.	God created the universe and all that is in it through direct action. This happened over a very short period of time, perhaps a calendar week. God did not use any indirect means or biological mechanisms to bring His creation into being, but used direct action or contact. In each of His acts of creation, God created the universe initially out of nothing (Gen. 1:1). From this universe he formed human beings and other parts of creation. Each species was created distinct from all others. God made man completely by a direct creative act and then created a woman also.
Presuppositions Regarding God and His Word	God does not exist and has never existed. The Bible has no validity for matters dealing with science.	God is one (not triune). He is eternal, infinitely good, wise, unchanging, perfect. However, He is not involved in the world miraculously. He does not reveal Himself other than in creation. Thus, the Bible is a human invention and only reflects the understanding of science and the world as understood by the people at the time of its writing.	God exists. The Bible is from God, but is not to be taken literally in every part. Science provides better understanding of matters relating to the origins of the world and development of life.	God is the one who is revealed in the Scriptures. His Word is considered to be the standard of truth, but is not to be taken literally in every part. The text of Genesis 1 provides for the solar days being non-contiguous days. God's creative activity should be understood without rejection of the great age of the universe and the earth accepted by many scientists.	God is the one who is revealed in the Scriptures. His Word is considered to be the standard of truth. The days of Genesis 1 are interpreted to be solar days contiguous to each other, contrary to the interpretation of empirical, or observable, data by many modern scientists. The earth is only a few thousand years old, in contrast to the great age accepted by many scientists.

Chart 61

	(View 1)	(View 2)	(View 3)	(View 4)	(View 5)
View of Mankind and God's Relationship with Mankind	Mankind is totally material. Death is final. Since there is no God, there is no relationship between man and God.	Mankind is the result of the evolutionary process. Although there is a God, God and mankind do not have a relationship.	While the physical body of humans is the result of the evolutionary process, their spiritual nature was created directly by God. The biblical doctrines regarding sin and redemption are valid, and humans can have a relationship with God through Jesus Christ.	Human beings are totally the result of a special creative act of God and can have a relationship with God through Jesus Christ.	Human beings are totally the result of a special creative act of God and can have a relationship with God through Jesus Christ.
Scientific Support	The evolutionary view is consistent with most of the scientific data. In general, it fits the fact that variation does take place now, sometimes through selection. This explains the effects of geographical isolation of various fauna and flora. *(spans views 1–3)*			This view fits with some of the scientific data—e.g., that variation takes place, the earth's age is great, development occurs within species, jumps within the fossil records are explained, humans are capable of speech.	This view fits the fact that the fossil record reveals a sudden appearance of a great variety of highly complex forms with no evident evolutionary ancestors. It also fits the fact that there are no transitional forms found in the fossil record. The second law of thermodynamics (involving entropy) supports this view.
Scientific Problems	There are several problems with the theory of evolution. One is that man does not fit the evolutionary model of adaptation; it would seem from the fossil record that man branched off quite early from the other animals. The fossil records indicate that man has been around for a long time. Moreover, evolution does not explain the human capability for language and speech. None of the "missing links" in the chain of evolutionary theory have been found, nor have any genuinely "good" mutations been found. *(spans views 1–3)*			There are no apparent scientific conflicts in this view if the Genesis account of creation is interpreted with long periods of time between creative acts (days) and if the creation account is primarily concerned with the creation of the earth but not the universe, since there is considerable time allowed for the days of Genesis 1 or between the creative acts of each of the first six days.	According to D. T. Gish, the biblical data do not contradict the scientific data that have been used to support the evolutionary theory.[1] Some see the main scientific problems in the areas of fossils (there are many life forms in fossils not present today) and the geographical distribution of plants and animals as difficult to explain from this view.

Chart 61

Main Views on the Origin of Life and of the Universe (continued)

	Naturalistic Evolution	Deistic Evolution	Theistic Evolution		
Biblical Support	The naturalistic evolutionary view flatly contradicts the biblical data that there is a God who created and sustains all things in the universe.	The deistic evolutionary view contradicts Scripture in that it holds to God as one (not triune), and that being a God who has withdrawn from involvement in the world. The Genesis account of creation indicates that God brought man into existence directly and distinctly and remains active in the world.	Theistic evolution conflicts with the teaching of Scripture if the opening chapters of Genesis are to be interpreted literally. Segraves says, "The creation of man from the dust followed by the creation of one woman from his side cannot be reconciled with any evolutionary origin of man without destroying the integrity of the language of the Bible."[2] Theistic evolution contradicts what Gen. 2:7 says—that man became a living being when God breathed into him the breath of life (man was already a living being)—unless that "breath of life" was a spiritual and not a physical endowment.	The biblical data supports this view as long as the days of Genesis 1 are interpreted as not contiguous and have for long periods of time between them.	This view fully fits the biblical data when the days are understood as solar days with no periods of time between each. There does not appear to be any indication in the Genesis text that there should be a great stretch of time between days. This view stands in contradiction to the interpretation by many scientists of empirical, or observable, data.
Summary	One issue at stake here for Christians is their view of God—their understanding of God's character and his relationship to the world. Those who believe in theistic evolution stress God's immanence and sovereignty. Those who believe in progressive or young earth creation stress God's transcendence and direct actions. Another issue is one's approach to hermeneutics and biblical interpretation.				
Bibliography	Brown, Walt. *In the Beginning: Compelling Evidence for Creation and the Flood.* 7th edition. Phoenix: Center for Scientific Creation, 2001. Burke, Derek, ed. *Creation and Evolution.* Leicester, U.K.: Inter-Varsity Press, 1985. Dawkins, Richard. *The Blind Watchmaker: Why the Evidence of Evolution Reveals a Universe Without Design.* London and New York: W. W. Norton, 1996. Erickson, Millard J. *Christian Theology.* Grand Rapids: Baker, 1985. Geisler, Norman L., and William D. Watkins. *Perspectives.* San Bernardino, Calif.: Here's Life, 1984. Heeren, Fred. *Show Me God.* Wheeling, Ill.: Searchlight, 1995. Jones, Steve, Robert Martin, and David Pilbeams, eds. *The Cambridge Encyclopedia of Human Evolution.* Cambridge, U.K.: Cambridge University Press, 1992. Klotz, John W. *Studies in Creation.* St. Louis: Concordia, 1985. Kofahl, Robert E., and Kelly L. Segraves. *The Creation Explanation.* Wheaton, Ill.: Harold Shaw, 1975. Moreland, J. P., and John Mark Reynolds, gen. eds. *Three Views on Creation and Evolution.* Grand Rapids: Zondervan, 1999. Newman, Robert C., and Herman J. Eckelmann Jr. *Genesis One and the Origin of the Earth.* Downers Grove, Ill.: InterVarsity Press, 1977. Reprint, Hatfield, Penn.: Interdisciplinary Biblical Research Institute, 1988. Van Till, Howard. *Portraits of Creation.* Grand Rapids: Eerdmans, 1990.				

Chart 61

[1] Derek Burke, ed., *Creation and Evolution* (Leicester, U.K.: Inter-Varsity Press, 1985), 192–97.

[2] Robert E. Kofahl and Kelly L. Segraves, *The Creation Explanation* (Wheaton, Ill.: Harold Shaw, 1975), 235–36.

Two Models of Origins: Fiat Creation and Naturalistic Evolution

There are two main models, or paradigms, to explain the origins of the universe and life: fiat creation (creation by command) and evolution. However, within these two models lies a variety of perspectives. Creationism may be understood to be recent or of great age, and the account of Genesis 1 may speak of the creation of both the universe and the earth or primarily of the earth. These acts of God under the creationist view are always creation by command, or fiat. The question of the age of the earth or universe is not generally viewed to be integral to the belief in creation. The more recently espoused view of origins called intelligent design is more narrowly and nonreligiously framed than earlier creation perspectives.

Evolution also may be seen from different angles, whether Darwinism, neo-Darwinism, or theistic evolution. The age of the universe and the earth is universally held among evolutionists as being billions of years old, a belief that is necessary to the evolution model. However, evolutionists holding to "punctuated equilibrium" believe that not all the transitions of life forms may have required the amount of time believed by classical Darwinists. In contrast to naturalistic evolutionists, theistic evolutionists believe in creation by command, but only in reference to a very few transitional forms and to the spiritual creation of the human.

Fiat Creation	Naturalistic Evolution
A Supreme Being brought matter into existence out of nothing and created various kinds of plants and animals, which have led to additional forms of largely the same kind through processes of genetics and environment. There is no crossing over of major divisions of plants or animals in the development of life.	The universe has always existed or began billions of years ago. The origin of matter is uncertain. Life began spontaneously. Humans ascended from lower animals by a natural process controlled totally by forces of nature.

Characteristics of the Two Models	
1. Theistic Views a Supreme Being (God) as the Originator and Creator of the universe and thus its Highest Being.	1. Humanistic Views nature as the originator and creator of the universe and man as its highest being.
2. Supernaturalistic Views the source of the universe as supernatural, the result of a direct act of a Supreme Being (God).	2. Naturalistic Views the source of the universe as entirely natural, the result of natural processes operating through time.
3. Design Attributes the systems and structures of the cosmos to a planned, purposive creation of all things in the beginning by an omniscient Creator.	3. Chance Attributes all systems and structures of the universe to the operation of natural processes under the impetus of innate properties of the universe. No external agent plans or directs these processes; the universe is self-contained and self-evolving by random actions of its components.
4. Man in God's Image Views the human species as a direct, special creation of God, made in God's image and likeness. Humans are qualitatively distinct from and superior to animals.	4. Man as Animal Views humans as a higher evolutionary form of animal, in essence not distinct from other animals. Although more than 98% of the genome makeup of mice is the same as that of humans, it is the "order" and "arrangement" (e.g., Satan vs. Santa) of the genome that make humans qualitatively distinct from and superior to animals.
5. Hebrew Scriptures Finds its source in the ancient cosmology of the Hebrew scriptures, in which God is viewed as separate from his creation. The biblical texts use the terms of other ancient cosmologies, but invest them with new meaning.	5. Mediterranean Cosmologies Finds its source in ancient Mediterranean nature religions (such as Enuma Elish), in which all things, including the gods, evolved out of water by natural processes.
6. Absolute Truth Views the Supreme Being (God) as transcending the universe He created and possessing complete knowledge of it. Therefore He is the basis for absolute truth and morality.	6. Relative Truth Views all things as constantly evolving, including truth and morality. Truth and morality are situational, based on what is practical and expedient, and are good only as they contribute to the evolution of life.

Chart 62

Two Models of Origins: Fiat Creation and Naturalistic Evolution (continued)

Predictions of the Two Models

1. Conservation Views the universe as completed upon creation, so the universe should be operating to conserve its order.	*1. Innovation* Views nature as constantly changing, moving toward higher levels of order. The universe should be creating new orders and processes.
2. Disintegration Views the universe as originally created perfect or complete, not lacking anything God intended. After the fall, the universe became subject to decay, with significant changes occurring in the direction of imperfection. The universe therefore demonstrates a tendency toward disorder and disintegration.	*2. Integration* Views the universe as continuing to change, giving rise to an increase in variety and higher levels of organization. The universe should demonstrate a tendency to integrate itself, to move to higher levels of order and complexity.
3. Catastrophism Views the earth as subject to the conservative processes of the universe. Major changes in the earth since creation are the result of catastrophes. The biblical creation model utilizes Noah's flood in this way. Earth history should be dominated by catastrophism.	*3. Uniformity* Views the universe as developing itself through natural processes operating in the same way that they do today. The earth's structures were all formed through the uniform operation of such natural processes.
4. Life from Life Views life as the direct result of a creative act and holds that organisms, upon creation, were given the ability to reproduce. Life can arise only from other life.	*4. Life from Nonlife* Views the entire universe, including life, as the product of natural processes. Nonliving chemicals and substances can in some way under certain circumstances give rise to life.
5. Fixed Kinds Views life as being created in discrete orders, capable of adaptation. Kinds are fixed, but are given the capacity to change within their kind as the environment demands (microevolution). There should be evidence of distinct gaps between kinds of life today and in the fossil record.	*5. Continuous Kinds* Views life as continually changing into higher orders of complexity and variety as a result of mutation and natural selection. Life not only evolves within kinds, but between them (macroevolution). Numerous transitional forms should be evident today and in the fossil record.
6. Natural Conservation Views the origin of the universe as completed with built-in conservation mechanism. Mutations are harmful. Natural selection is used to eliminate such mutations.	*6. Natural Creation* Views the origin of the universe as ongoing, constantly attaining new levels of order. Mutations can be beneficial, resulting in new life forms through natural selection.
7. Old Earth Is Not Necessary According to most evolutionists, an old earth is a necessary condition for the evolution of kinds to take place, thus excluding the possibility of a young earth to fit the evolutionary model. However, the biblical position of creation out of nothing (*ex nihilo*) can fit within either a young or old age dating scheme, since reality and life-form systems were created fully formed without the need to evolve over long periods of time.	*7. Old Earth Is Necessary* According to most evolutionists, an old earth is a necessary condition for the evolution of kinds to take place. Evolution requires vast amounts of time for natural processes to have developed the order and complexity of the present universe. The earth is immensely old (5 billion years), with the universe being billions of years older.

Chart 62

Christian Theories of Origins

Theory	Gap Theory	Pictorial Day Theory	Ideal-Time Theory	Flood Geology
Variant Names	Restitution Progressive-Creative-Catastrophism Creation-Ruination-Recreation	Framework Hypothesis Revelation Day Moderate Concordism	Apparent Age Pro-Chronic	Young Earth Creationism
Source	Thomas Chalmers	J. H. Kurtz Hugh Miller	Philip Henry Gosse	George McCready Price
Adherents	Cyrus I. Scofield Donald Grey Barnhouse Erich Sauer Harry Rimmer	Bernard Ramm	Henry M. Morris John Whitcomb	H. W. Clark Henry M. Morris Byron Nelson Alfred M. Rehwinkel John Whitcomb
Features	This view postulates an original creation that was catastrophically marred and then "remodeled" by God in six literal days. The hiatus between these two events is undetermined but held to be a long period of time. An extensive development of Satanology is peculiar to this theory in connection with the catastrophe. The theory allows for the geologic ages to occur during the gap.	This theory holds that the six "days" of Gen. 1 correspond to a succession of normal days in Moses' life during which he received information regarding God's prior creative work. This theory adduces a combined chronological/logical ordering of Gen. 1. It is amenable to a flexible/protracted chronology, matching geological periods.	This view states that God created the earth in six literal days, fashioning all things with an apparent (ideal) age considerably greater than their actual age. Thus rocks had layers, trees had rings, etc., at creation's inception. This view refutes the concept of a much older earth as proposed by evolutionary uniformitarianism.	The Noahic diluvium covered the earth with waves of incalculable velocity, resulting in rock strata *suggestive* of billions of years but, in reality, mere indicators of the unusual violence of the Noahic catastrophe (a mere space of one year). Hence, this theory asserts the earth's age to correspond to literal Bible chronology (including a six-day creation).
Theological and/or Exegetical Pivot	In Gen. 1 a distinction is made between the Hebrew words *bara* (creative) and *asah* (remaking). Interprets the 1st *waw* of Gen. 1:2 as "then" instead of "now." Interprets *hayetha* of 1:2 as "became" instead of "was."	The overwhelming religious intent of the entire creation narrative.	The Adam of Gen. 1:27; 2:7 was not introduced to the Edenic milieu as an infant but rather as an ideally adapted human in full maturity.	The totality of the Genesis 6 flood and concomitant time-compressed ordering of geological strata supports a literalist Gen. 1 chronology.
Suggested Age of Earth	Several billion years.	Several billion years.	Only a few thousand years.	Only a few thousand years.
Bibliography	Allison, Mark, and David Patton, eds. *Another Time, Another Place, Another Man: A Biblical Alternative to the Traditional View of Creation.* Lawrenceville, Ga.: Dake, 1997. Pember, G. H. *Earth's Earliest Ages.* Reprint, Grand Rapids: Kregel, 1987.	Hagopian, David G., ed. *The Genesis Debate: Three Views on the Days of Creation.* Peabody, Mass.: Global, 2000. Kline, Meredith G. "Space and Time in the Genesis Cosmogony." *www.asa3.org/ASA/PSCF3-96Kline.html.* Ramm, Bernard. *The Christian View of Science and Scripture.* Grand Rapids: Eerdmans, 1955. 173–229.	Gosse, Philip H. *Omphalos.* Reprint, Woodbridge, Conn.: Ox Bow. 1999. Morris, Henry M., ed. *Scientific Creationism.* 2nd ed. Green Forest, Ark.: Master, 1974.	Whitcomb, John C. *The Genesis Flood: The Biblical Record and Its Scientific Implications.* Nutley, N.J.: Presbyterian & Reformed, 1960. Woodmorappe, John. *Studies in Flood Geology: A Compilation of Research Studies Supporting Creation and the Flood.* El Cajon, Calif: Institute of Creation Research, 2000.

Chart 63

Christian Theories of Origins (continued)

Theory	Local Creation Theory	Day-Age Theory	Progressive Creationism	Theistic Evolution
Variant Names	Eden-Only	Divine Day and Concordism	Old Earth Creationism	Evolutionary Creationism
Source	John Pye Smith	John William Dawson James Dwight Dana	Charles Lyell	Charles Babbage Alfred Russel Wallace
Adherents	John H. Sailhamer	Gleason Archer William Bell Riley William Jennings Bryan	Millard J. Erickson Norman L. Geisler Robert C. Newman John Mark Reynolds	C. S. Lewis Pierre Tielhard de Chardin Stanley Jaki Howard Van Till Richard H. Bube
Features	Contends that the (literal) six-day creative account of Gen. 1 was confined to the immediate area of the garden of Eden, and literal biblical chronology applies only to that region. Geology and biology are thus at liberty to (scientifically) arrive at the age for the rest of the planet, and theology (supernatural) and science (natural) are given equal time.	Alleges that God, in successive acts corresponding to six metaphorical days in Gen. 1, created the earth over an extremely protracted period of time. Each of the creation days was a long period of time but contiguous with the others. The geological and fossil evidences reflect the sequence of the creation.	Maintains that the six days of creation are solar days with long periods of time between each of them. Thus there are multi-million-year periods of earth history in which things remain mostly the same, punctuated by bursts of divine creative activity.	Claims that God used an evolutionary process to successively create all the forms of life that have existed during earth's history. Sometimes it is said that the first single-celled organism was created *ex nihilo*, while every creature subsequent to it evolved by natural processes.
Theological and/or Exegetical Pivot	"The earth" in Gen. 1:2 refers only to "that portion ... assigned for the habitation of mankind" (Smith).	Non-literal interpretation of the Hebrew word for day (*yom*) in Gen. 1.	Natural revelation (the findings of empirical science) provides a partial basis for interpreting the Bible.	A commitment to the view that special revelation (Scripture) and general revelation (nature) are compatible, although the evaluation and interpretation of the first (theology and biblical studies) and the second (science) may not always agree.
Suggested Age of Earth	*Eden*: a few millennia *Rest of earth*: several billion years.	Several billion years.	Several billion years.	Several billion years.
Bibliography	Martin, Timothy. "Beyond Creation Science" at *www. truthinliving.org/Book/Ch%207. htm.* Smith, John Pye. *On the Relation Between the Holy Scriptures and Some Parts of Geological Science.* London: Henry G. Bohm, reprint of 3rd ed. of 1843. Sailhamer, John H. *Genesis Unbound: A Provocative New Look at the Creation Account.* Eugene, Ore.: Multnomah, 1996.	Hagopian, David G., ed. *The Genesis Debate: Three Views on the Days of Creation.* Peabody, Mass.: Global, 2000. Deem, Rich. "Day-Age Genesis One Interpretation" at *www.godandscience. org/apologetics/day-age.html.*	Pun, Pattle P. T. "A Theology of Progressive Creationism." *Journal of the American Scientific Affiliation* 39, no. 1 (March 1987). Ross, Hugh. *A Matter of Days: Resolving a Creation Controversy.* Colorado Springs: NavPress, 2004. Erickson, Millard J. *Christian Theology.* Grand Rapids: Baker, 1983. Vol. 1:380–82.	Falk, Darrel R. *Coming to Peace with Science: Bridging the Worlds Between Faith and Biology.* Downers Grove, Ill.: InterVarsity, 2004. Miller, Kenneth R. *Finding Darwin's God: A Scientist's Search for Common Ground Between God and Evolution.* New York: Harper Perennial, 2000. Tielhard de Chardin, Pierre. *The Phenomenon of Man.* New York: Harper, 1965. Van Till, Howard. *The Fourth Day: What the Bible and the Heavens Are Telling Us about Creation.* Grand Rapids: Eerdmans, 1986.

Additional Bibliography:
Moreland, J. P., and John Mark Reynolds, eds. *Three Views on Creation and Evolution.* Grand Rapids: Zondervan, 1999.
Smith, Charles R. *Is There a Gap Between Genesis 1:1 and 1:2?* Master's Thesis, Dallas Theological Seminary, 1966. Chaps. 1–2.
Tenney, Merrill C., ed. *Zondervan Pictorial Encyclopedia of the Bible.* Grand Rapids: Zondervan, 1980. Vol. 1:982–89.
Youngblood, Ronald, ed. *The Genesis Debate.* Nashville: Thomas Nelson, 1986.

Chart 63

Scientific Evidence for the Age of the Universe

	Arguments for Old Universe	Arguments for Recent Universe
Thermodynamics	Thermodynamics is not a reliable determinant for the age of the universe since the universe is an open system.	The second law of thermodynamics proves that the universe is not billions of years old because it is decaying at a rate that allows for only thousands of years.
Astronomy	Uniform expansion of the universe extrapolates back to a beginning about 10 billion years ago.	• The expansion of the universe seems to be slowing down. • The average lifetime of a comet is 10,000 years, and since many comets still exist, the solar system is probably less than 50,000 years old. • The stability of Saturn's rings indicates they are less than 100,000 years old. • The depth of moon dust extrapolates back to a period of meteorite bombardment of less than 20,000 years.
Geology	• The measured worldwide uniform rate of sedimentation extrapolates back to formation of rocks about 600 million years ago. • The geologic column can be dated by index fossils to about 3 billion years. • Uniform deposition of uranium salts into the oceans extrapolates back to the age of the oceans of about 1 million years.	• A worldwide flood could have deposited all known sedimentation in a two-year period 5,000 years ago. • Volcanoes have spewed forth enough water in the last 100,000 years to fill the oceans. • The influx of helium-4 into the atmosphere extrapolates back to birth of the atmosphere about 10,000 years ago. • The amount of meteorite dust on the surface of the earth argues for an age of less than 100,000 years. • The volume of lava deposited on the earth's crust and the rate of volcanic activity argue for origin of the earth 10,000 years ago. • High oil pressures in deep deposits require sudden burial less than 10,000 years ago.
Radiometric Dating	• Carbon 14 has dated animal and plant specimens as old as 1,000 to 1 billion years. • Periodic modification of decay rates by natural catastrophes has set the beginning of life at about 1 billion years ago.	• Experiments have shown that carbon 14 dating is accurate back to only about 1500 BC. • Experiments have shown that potassium-argon dating has a 50 percent probability of error.
Physics		The present rate of decay of the earth's magnetic field extrapolates back to a maximum age of the earth of 10,000 years.
Age of Universe	4.5 billion to 20 billion years	Generally 6,000 to 20,000 years

Bibliography:
Froede, Carl. *Field Studies in Catastrophic Geology*. St. Joseph, Mo.: Creation Research Society, 1998.
Lammerts, Walter E. *Why Not Creation?* St. Joseph, Mo.: Creation Research Society, 1970.
Morris, Henry M. *The Genesis Record*. Grand Rapids: Baker, 1976.
Morris, Henry M., William W. Boardman, Jr., and Robert F. Koontz. *Science and Creation*. San Diego: Creation-Science Research Center, 1973.
Morris, John. *The Young Earth*. Green Forest, Ark.: Master, 1994.
———. *Biblical Cosmology and Modern Science*. Phillipsburg, N.J.: Presbyterian & Reformed, 1970.
Newman, Robert C., and Herman J. Eckelmann Jr. *Genesis One and the Origin of the Earth*. Reprint, Hatfield, Penn.: Interdisciplinary Biblical Research Institute, 1988.
Ross, Hugh. *Creation and Time*. Colorado Springs: NavPress, 1994.
Slusher, Harold S. *Age of the Cosmos*. El Cajon, Calif.: Institute for Creation Research, 1980.
Young, Davis A. *Christianity and the Age of the Earth*. Ashland, Oreg.: Artisan Press, 1988.
Vardiman, Larry. *Sea-Floor Sediment and the Age of the Earth*. Dexter, Mich.: Thomson-Shore: 1996.
Vardiman, Larry, A. A. Snelling, and E. F. Chaffin. *Radioisotopes and the Age of the Earth*. El Cajon, Calif.: Institute for Creation Research, 2000.
———. *Radioisotopes and the Age of the Earth*. El Cajon, Calif.: Institute for Creation Research, 2005.

Chart 64

Contrasts between Origin Science and Operation Science

Origin Science	Operation Science
"Origin Science" refers to empirical, or observable, evidence (and inferences from that evidence) that relates to theories regarding the origins of the universe and biological life. It deals with singular, unobserved, unrepeatable events.	"Operation Science" refers to those scientific methods, procedures, and sets of data used in studying ongoing processes. It deals with regular, observable, repeatable events.
Features 1. Attempts to determine first causes 2. Concerns singularities 3. Concerns unobservable events 4. Hypotheses cannot be tested directly 5. Employs forensic methods of inquiry 6. Does not rely upon operational laws 7. Does not involve direct observation 8. Does not engage in repeatable experiments (except in those cases where the experiment provides indirect confirmation for the theory in question)	*Features* 1. Describes how things function 2. Concerns regularities 3. Concerns observable events 4. Hypotheses can be tested directly 5. Employs empirical methods of inquiry 6. Relies upon operational laws 7. Involves direct observation 8. Engages in repeatable experiments

Note: The terms *origin science* and *operation science* probably first appear in Charles B. Thaxton, Walter L. Bradley, and Roger L. Olsen, *The Mystery of Life's Origin* (New York: Philosophical Library, 1984).

Source: Norman L. Geisler and J. Kerby Anderson, *Origin Science: A Proposal for the Creation-Evolution Controversy* (Grand Rapids: Baker, 1987).

Chart 65

The Relationship between Creation Ex Nihilo and Evangelical Theology

Fields of Study	Theological Inferences
Bibliology	If the Bible teaches creation ex nihilo and if naturalistic evolution is accepted as true, then the Bible cannot also be true. If the Bible is not true in its entirety, then it cannot be the inerrant Word of God. If the Bible is not the Word of God, then it is not necessarily authoritative.
Anthropology	The doctrine of creation ex nihilo includes the origin of man as a distinct life form. The Bible teaches that "God created man in His own image; in the image of God He created him; male and female He created them" (Gen. 1:29). "And the LORD God formed man of the dust of the ground, and breathed into his nostrils the breath of life, and man became a living being" (Gen. 2:7). Furthermore, the Bible teaches that man was made "very good" (Gen. 1:31) and became worse. Naturalistic evolution teaches that man was worse and has been getting better.
Hamartiology	The origin and nature of sin are closely linked with a literal interpretation of the creation account of man in Genesis 1–2. Apart from this account, the origin and nature of sin are much more difficult to understand theologically. The Bible teaches that man was made good (Gen. 1:31) and upright (Eccl. 7:29), but that man sinned against God (Gen. 7:6) and passed sin onto all men (Rom. 5:12).
Soteriology	The doctrine of salvation is related to the doctrine of creation ex nihilo. The Bible states, "He chose us in Him before the foundation of the world" (Eph. 1:4). If there is no creation ex nihilo, then the predetermined redemptive plan of God is also in question. If the doctrine of creation ex nihilo is altered, the doctrine of salvation will not go unchanged. Soteriology demands creation ex nihilo.
Pneumatology	The Holy Spirit is recorded as having a significant supervising and organizing work throughout the six days of creation. The Bible teaches that "the earth was without form and void; and darkness was on the face of the deep. And the Spirit of God was hovering over the face of the waters" (Gen. 1:2). "You send forth your Spirit, they are created" (Ps. 104:30). "The Spirit of God has made me, and the breath of the Almighty gives me life" (Job 33:4). One of the great works of the Holy Spirit is that of creation. Pneumatology demands creation ex nihilo.
Eschatology	The doctrine of creation ex nihilo is also closely linked with the doctrine of future things, or end-time events. "Where is this 'coming' he promised? Ever since our fathers died, everything goes on as it has since the beginning of creation" (2 Peter 3:4 NIV). The doctrine of future things demands creation ex nihilo.
Angelology	The Bible clearly teaches that angels were created ex nihilo. "Praise Him, all his angels;… Let them praise the name of the LORD, For He commanded and they were created" (Ps. 148:2–5). "For by Him all things were created that are in heaven and that are on earth, visible and invisible, whether thrones or … powers. All things were created through Him and for Him" (Col 1:16). Both holy and fallen angels were created ex nihilo. They are not eternal beings, neither did they evolve.
Christology	Surely the doctrine of Christ is central to the Christian faith. If a denial of the doctrine of creation ex nihilo would bring down the doctrine of Christ, then that denial would also bring down the Christian faith. Jesus believed and taught the doctrine of creation ex nihilo. Either creation is true or Jesus is a liar. If creation ex nihilo is not true, then the whole Christian system crumbles. Christianity demands creation ex nihilo.

Adapted from class notes of Norman L. Geisler, instructor for 401, Bibliology and Prolegomena.

Chart 66

Intelligent Design Theory

Definition	Intelligent design is a scientific theory originating in the late 1980s that has its roots in information theory (i.e., measurement of data, essential to things like physics, computers, and engineering) and observations about intelligent action. Intelligent design theorists maintain that information and specified complexity as found in biological systems (e.g., DNA or bacteria flagellum) are best accounted for as a product of design by an intelligent agent. No explicit statements are made about the identity of the intelligent designer. The theory merely says that intelligent action was involved at some points with the origins of various aspects of biological life. Intelligent design theory holds that certain features of the universe and living things are best explained by an intelligent cause and are not the result of an undirected, chance-based process such as Darwinian evolution. Even the atheistic zoologist Richard Dawkins says that intuitively, "Biology is the study of complicated things that give the appearance of having been designed for a purpose" (*The Blind Watchmaker*, 1). Darwinists hold that natural selection did the "designing." However, intelligent design theorist Stephen C. Meyer notes, "In all cases where we know the causal origin of 'high information content,' experience has shown that intelligent design played a causal role" (*DNA and Other Designs*). Intelligent design implies that life exists as a result of the purposeful action of an intelligent designer. This is in stark contrast to Darwinian evolution, which postulates that life is the product of and can be explained by natural processes alone—that life is merely the result of time plus chance plus matter changed by the purposeless blind forces of nature.	
Terms	**Creationism**	The belief that all life, the earth, and the entire universe were created by a supernatural agent sometime in the past.
	Darwinism	"Each life form has certain random mutations that make it either more or less fit to survive in a given environment. Over time, these random mutations create the vast array of life forms that we see, from sponges to elephants to people. There is no need for design. This was Charles Darwin's explanation of evolution" (Denyse O'Leary, *By Design or by Chance?* 9).
	Evolution	"The theory that all life forms are descended from one or several common ancestors that were present on the early earth, three to four billion years ago" (Ibid., 9).
	Irreducible Complexity	"A biological system is irreducibly complex when its operation requires the cooperation of numerous parts, none of which performs a useful function unless all are present" (Ibid., 185).
	Macroevolution (Macromutation)	Major evolutionary transition from one type of organism to another occurring at the level of the species and higher taxa. The "origin and diversification of higher taxa" (Douglas Futuyma, *Evolutionary Biology*). "Evolutionary change on a grand scale, encompassing [among other things] *the origin of novel designs*" (Neil Campbell and Jane Reece, *Biology*, 4th ed.).
	Microevolution (Micromutation)	Evolutionary change involving the gradual accumulation of mutation leading to new variation within a species. "Slight, short-term evolutionary changes within species" (Futuyma, *Evolutionary Biology*).
Implications of Evolutionism	**Richard Dawkins, zoologist**	"Although atheism might have been logically tenable before Darwin, Darwin made it possible to be an intellectually fulfilled atheist" (Dawkins, *The Blind Watchmaker*).

Chart 67

Intelligent Design Theory (continued)

	William B. Provine, biologist	"Naturalistic evolution has clear consequences that Charles Darwin understood perfectly: 1) No gods worth having exist; 2) no life after death exists; 3) no ultimate foundation for ethics exists; 4) no ultimate meaning in life exists; and 5) human free will is nonexistent (Provine, "Evolution: Free Will and Punishment and Meaning in Life").
	Stephen Jay Gould, paleontologist	"We are here because one odd group of fishes had a peculiar fin anatomy that could transform into legs for terrestrial creatures;… *We may yearn for a 'higher' answer—but none exists*" (Gould, in *The Meaning of Life*, emphasis added).
	George Gaylord Simpson, paleontologist	"Man is the result of a *purposeless* and *natural process* that did not have him in mind" (Simpson, *The Meaning of Evolution*, 345, emphasis added).
	Edward Wilson, socio-biologist	"Life … has arisen by evolution…. The human brain and all its activities have arisen from the same…. *No more complicated explanation is needed to account for human existence, either scientifically or spiritually*" (Wilson, in *The Meaning of Life*, emphasis added).

Intelligent Design and the Scientific Method

1. Observation	The ways that intelligent agents act can be observed in the natural world and described. When intelligent agents act, it can be observed that they produce high levels of "complex-specified information" (CSI). CSI is detected by the following criteria: the event is unlikely to happen (i.e., complex) and conforms to a pattern (i.e., specified). Language and machines are examples of things with high levels of CSI. From our observation of the world, these high levels of CSI are always the product of intelligent design.
2. Hypothesis	If living organisms are the result of an intelligent agent, then we should be able to examine them and find the same high levels of CSI in these organisms that we find in human-designed languages and machines.
3. Experiment	We can examine biological structures to test if high CSI exists. When we look at natural objects in biology, we find many machine-like structures that are *specified*, because they have a particular arrangement of parts that is necessary for them to function, and *complex*, because they have an unlikely arrangement of many interacting parts. These biological machines are "irreducibly complex," for any change in the nature or arrangement of these parts would destroy their function. Irreducibly complex structures cannot be built up through an alternative theory, such as Darwinian evolution, because Darwinian evolution requires that a biological structure be functional along every small step of its evolution. "Reverse engineering" of these structures shows that they cease to function if changed even slightly.
4. Conclusion	Because biological structures exhibit high levels of CSI, a quality that is produced only by intelligent design, and because there is no other known mechanism to explain the origin of these "irreducibly complex" biological structures, we conclude that they were intelligently designed and not the result of Darwinian evolution.

Chart 67

Intelligent Design Distinguished from Scientific Creationism
How does intelligent design differ from the older scientific creationism?

Accepting intelligent design entails an acceptance of "creationism," which is conceived broadly enough to be consistent with an "old" earth (the current scientific estimate of around 4.6 billion years), or with theistic evolution (i.e., an intelligent agent guiding the process of evolution) and a "young" earth (6,000 to 20,000 years old).

Intelligent design is more theologically diverse than scientific creationism (whether young or old earth), which is usually propounded by fundamentalist and/or evangelical Christians. Contributors to the seminal volume *Mere Creation* represent diverse theological beliefs: John Mark Reynolds (Eastern Orthodox Church), Jonathan Wells (Unification Church), David Berlinski (Judaism), and Michael Behe (Roman Catholic Church).

Intelligent design, which offers a bona fide research program in science, should be recognized as a distinct movement in contemporary science. It should not be casually lumped together with the earlier-espoused scientific creationism under the general rubric of "creationism."

Intelligent Design Compared with and Distinguished from Evolution
Most of the primary postulates of Darwinism accepted by most scientists are not affected by intelligent design theory.

Alike	1. Variation exists within members of the same species. A species is a group of interbreeding animals or plants. 2. Variation can be inherited. That is, parents pass on their traits to their offspring. 3. Resources like food, water, and shelter are limited. Animals and plants compete for these limited resources. 4. Natural selection is a direct consequence of the first three tenets. Darwin proposed that since natural resources are limited, individuals with favorable traits are more likely to survive and reproduce. Because these individuals pass on favorable traits to their descendants, nature selects life with favorable characteristics and preserves it. Darwin called this process "natural selection" or "survival of the fittest."
Different	(Darwin's first four tenets are verified by scientific experiments, but the fifth is only speculation and extrapolation. Evolution creates diversity, but not complexity.) 5. Under the guidance of natural selection, simple life evolved into complex life. Since large evolutionary changes are too slow to be observed directly in scientific experiments, Darwin could not test this tenet. So instead, he extrapolated. He documented the small changes that can occur from one generation to the next, and proposed that through numerous, successive, slight modifications, guided by natural selection, the descendants of simple animals evolved into complex animals" (Stuart Pullen, *Evolution vs. Intelligent Design*).
Tenets of Intelligent Design Theory	1. The information needed for life is contained in a molecule known as DNA. This information can be analyzed with a field of science called "information theory" and with systems biology (Leroy Hood). 2. The complexity of a life is a measure of the information in its DNA. Information and complexity are synonyms. 3. Natural selection does not create information, it only modifies existing information. Thus, new information must be created by genetic drift-random changes to DNA. 4. The odds associated with events in the past (such as the origin and evolution of life) can be accurately determined using information and probability theory. 5. If the odds associated with the origin and evolution of life are too small, then design is implicated, and it may be inferred (*www.discovery.org/csc/*).

Chart 67

Intelligent Design Theory (continued)

Parts of this chart were adapted from *The Idea Center* website *www.ideacenter.org*.

Bibliography

Behe, Michael J. *Darwin's Black Box: The Biochemical Challenge to Evolution*. New York: Free Press, 1996.

Campbell, Neil A., and Jane B. Reece. *Biology*. 4th edition. Boston: Benjamin Cummings, 2002.

Dawkins, Richard. *The Blind Watchmaker*. 1986. Reprint, New York: Norton, 1991.

Dembski, William A. *Intelligent Design: The Bridge Between Science and Theology*. Downers Grove, Ill.: InterVarsity Press, 1999.

Dembski, William A., ed. *Mere Creation: Science, Faith and Intelligent Design*. Downers Grove, Ill.: InterVarsity Press, 1998.

Friend, David, ed. *The Meaning of Life*. Boston: Little, Brown, 1991.

Futuyma, Douglas J. *Evolutionary Biology*. 3rd edition. Sunderland, Mass.: Sinauer Associates, 2006.

House, H. Wayne. "Darwinism and the Law: Can Non-Naturalistic Scientific Theories Survive Constitutional Challenge?" *Regent University Law Review* 13, no. 2 (2000–2001).

Meyer, Stephen C. "DNA and Other Designs." *First Things* 102 (April 2000).

O'Leary, Denyse. *By Design or by Chance? The Growing Controversy on the Origins of Life in the Universe*. Kitchener, Ontario: Castle Quay, 2004.

Provine, William B. "Evolution: Free Will and Punishment and Meaning in Life." Address, University of Tennesssee at Knoxville, 12 February 1998. http://fp.bio.utk.edu/DarwinDayProvineAddress.htm.

Pullen, Stuart. *Evolution vs. Intelligent Design*. 1 January 2001. www.theory-of-evolution.net/introduction.pdf.

Simpson, George Gaylord. *The Meaning of Evolution*. Revised edition. New Haven, Conn.: Yale University Press, 1967.

Woodward, Thomas. *Doubts about Darwin: A History of Intelligent Design*. Grand Rapids: Baker, 2003.

Chart 67

Intelligent and Unintelligent Causes Contrasted

Things Requiring an Intelligent Cause	Things Not Requiring an Intelligent Cause
Proponents of Intelligent Design posit that certain things require an intelligent cause to account for the object's "specified complexity." According to William A. Dembski, if a thing is observed to exhibit specified complexity, then one can make the justified inference that an intelligent agent designed the thing in question. Specified complexity is found in objects that display both (1) a large amount of precisely stipulated information and (2) intricacy of structure. Example: "A single letter of the alphabet is specified without being complex. A long sentence of random letters is complex without being specified. A Shakespearean sonnet is both complex and specified." The following chart offers examples of objects requiring an intelligent cause and objects that do not.	
1. Stained-glass window	1. Formation of fragments in a pile of broken glass
2. Arrowhead	2. Round stone
3. Sand castle	3. Sand dunes
4. Airplane	4. Metal, rubber, glass, and other raw materials strewn about a junkyard
5. Crystal chandelier	5. Crystal
6. A coherent paragraph written in the English language	6. A random series of letters (in the English alphabet), spaces, and punctuation marks
Source: William A. Dembski and James M. Kushiner, eds., *Signs of Intelligence: Understanding Intelligent Design* (Grand Rapids: Brazos, 2001).	

Chart 68